DrawPlus X2
Resource Guide

This book has been created and output in entirety using Serif PagePlus

Contacting Serif

Contacting Serif technical support

Technical support is provided by telephone and our Web support page, and useful information can be obtained via our web-based forums (see below).

UK Technical Support	(0845) 345 6770 (local rate, UK only)
	http://www.support.serif.com/
International Technical Support	(+44 (115) 914 9090
	http://www.support.serif.com/
USA Technical Support	(603) 886-6642
	http://www.support.serif.com/

Please do not fax technical support queries.

Additional contact information

World Wide Web:

Serif Web Site	http://www.serif.com
Forums	http://www.serif.com/forums.asp
Serif Newsgroups	news://news.serif.com

Main office (UK, Europe):

The Software Centre, PO Box 2000, Nottingham, NG11 7GW, UK

Main:	(0115) 914 2000
Registration (UK only):	(0800) 376 1989
Sales (UK only):	(0800) 376 7070
Customer Service (UK only)	(0845) 345 6770 (local rate, UK only)
Customer Service (International):	(0115) 914 9090
General Fax:	(0115) 914 2020

North American office (USA, Canada):

The Software Center, 13 Columbia Drive, Suite 5, Amherst NH 03031, USA

Main:	(603) 889-8650
Registration:	(800) 794-6876
Sales:	(800) 55-SERIF or 557-3743
Customer Service:	(800) 489-6720
General Fax:	(603) 889-1127

International enquiries:

Please contact our main office.

Contents

Introduction

Welcome to the DrawPlus X2 Resource Guide!

Whether you are new to DrawPlus or a seasoned graphic artist, the DrawPlus Resource Guide offers content to help you get the best out of DrawPlus. From a range of novice and professional tutorials to get you started or to help accomplish a complex project, to full-colour previews of DrawPlus's design templates, samples, Gallery elements, and more, the Resource Guide is something you will return to time and time again.

About the Resource Guide

The Resource Guide is your key to getting even more out of DrawPlus and is organized into the following chapters.

- **Tutorials:** Step-by-step training to introduce you to essential tools and techniques, and show you how to tackle some interesting projects. (You'll find additional tutorials and projects on the DrawPlus Program CD and Resource CD.)
- **DrawPlus Gallery:** Lists the content included in the DrawPlus X2 Gallery available on the Program CD and the Resource CD.
- **Design Templates:** A useful gallery of all the Design Templates available with the Resource CD.
- **Design Elements:** Shows some of the Design Elements available in DrawPlus X2.
- **Samples:** Examples of what you can do with DrawPlus X2.

How the Resource Guide was made

This full-colour Resource Guide was created and output using PagePlus, employing many PagePlus features. These include:
- **BookPlus** to unify separate publications with a common page numbering system.
- **Mail and Photo Merge with Repeating Areas** to automatically create pages with picture content based on a folder of images.
- The comprehensive **Find and Replace** functionality to apply text styles consistently (and quickly) throughout.

Finally, each chapter has been incorporated into a PagePlus Book comprised of multiple publication 'chapters,' and has been published as a press-ready PDF, accurately maintaining all text, fonts, images, and native colouring, all in a suitable CMYK colour format for professional printing.

Tutorials

Welcome to the Serif DrawPlus X2 Tutorials

These tutorials include material for beginners as well as more experienced DrawPlus users.

If you're new to DrawPlus, we suggest you start with the **Level 1** tutorials. These step-by-step exercises introduce you to the program and allow you to experiment with basic creative tools and techniques. Topics such as shapes, lines, fills, filter effects, and the natural media brushes are explored.

In addition to the **Level 1** tutorials, we also offer the following:

- **Level 2 Tutorials**—These tutorials are intermediate-level exercises that aim to boost your mastery of DrawPlus tools and allow you to further experiment with more advanced creative techniques.

- **Drawing Projects**—The DrawPlus Projects reinforce the use of multiple tools and provide a problem/solution approach to creative design challenges.

- **Animation Projects**—The Animation Projects demonstrate stopframe and keyframe animation techniques, with emphasis on the new functionality introduced with DrawPlus X2. These projects vary in complexity from beginner to advanced level.

Accessing the tutorials
You can access the tutorials in one of the following ways:

- From the DrawPlus StartUp Wizard, under **View**, click **Tutorials**.

- From DrawPlus, click **Help** and then click **Tutorials**.

Accessing the sample files
To access the sample files that are referred to in the tutorials, browse to the **Workspace** folder in your DrawPlus installation. Usually, you'll find this folder in the following location:

C:\Program Files\Serif\DrawPlus\X2\Tutorials\Workspace.

The tutorials are presented as PDF files, which you can print out or view onscreen. If you prefer to view the tutorials onscreen, you can quickly switch between DrawPlus and the tutorial document by pressing **Alt + Tab**.

Use the Natural Media Brushes

DrawPlus provides you with an exciting range of possibilities for creating natural looking artistic effects. The **Brushes** tab contains a vast array of pressure-sensitive brush strokes—a powerful set of tools that dramatically expands your potential for creativity by allowing you to create effects such as pencil sketches, charcoal drawings, and watercolours.

In this tutorial, we'll introduce you to this exciting collection of drawing tools and show you how you can use them to create natural-looking effects with ease.

You'll learn how to:

- Use the **Brushes** tab, **Paintbrush** tool, **Brush** context toolbar, and **Pressure** tab.

- Apply and edit brush strokes using the mouse.

- Apply and edit brush strokes using a pen tablet—an electronic pad equipped with a cordless pen.

- Change brush stroke attributes such as width, colour, smoothness, and opacity.

- Set brush stroke defaults.

- Adjust the pressure-sensitivity and pressure profile of your brush strokes.

Use the Natural Media Brushes

The brush styles provided on the DrawPlus **Brushes** tab are intended to mimic the strokes created by 'real' paintbrushes, pens, pencils, and charcoal crayons. This means that when you select a particular brush, you should use it in the same way you would use the traditional art medium it represents.

The aim of this tutorial is to show you how to use the brushes in your drawings. We'll demonstrate a couple of techniques and illustrate how you can create different effects by adjusting brush stroke style and attributes.

Let's start by exploring the various tabs, tools, and controls that you'll be using:

- The **Brushes** tab
- The **Paintbrush** tool
- The **Brush context toolbar**
- The **Pressure** tab

> 💡 DrawPlus provides a large selection of default brushes. However, you can also create your own custom brushes and add them to the **Brushes** tab.
>
> See the Level 2 tutorial, "Make Your Own Brushes," on the DrawPlus X2 Resource CD.

The Brushes tab

Use the **Brushes** tab to select the natural media effect you want to use. DrawPlus provides over 200 different brush styles from which to choose. Brush styles are divided into categories, each of which provides a different natural media effect—Pencil, Charcoal, Watery Paint, Dry Paint, and so on. Simply select a category from the drop-down list and then click a brush style swatch. Once you have chosen your brush style you can:

- Adjust the width of your stroke—on the **Line** tab, type a value or drag the slider. (Note that if the **Paintbrush** tool is the active tool, you can also set the brush width on the **Brush context toolbar**. See the following sections.)

- Change the colour of your brush stroke—at the top left of the **Swatches** or **Colour** tab, click to activate the **Line** option and then click a colour to apply it.

The Paintbrush tool

Select the **Paintbrush** tool to apply a brush stroke from the **Brushes** tab.

To use the Paintbrush tool

1 On the Drawing toolbar, click the **Paintbrush** tool.

2 On the **Brushes** tab, in the brush category drop-down list, select the category you want to use.

3 In the brush style list, click the swatch of the style you want to use.

4 Use your mouse or pen and tablet to apply the brush stroke to your page.

Use the Natural Media Brushes

To draw and edit brush strokes using a mouse

- To create a brush stroke, click where you want the brush stroke to start and then hold the mouse button down as you paint. The stroke appears immediately and follows your mouse movements.

- To end the brush stroke, release the mouse button.

- To extend the brush stroke, select the stroke with the **Paintbrush**, then position the mouse cursor over one of the stroke end nodes. The cursor changes to include a plus symbol. Click on the node and drag to add a new segment.

- To redraw any part of the stroke, select it with the ⟨⟩ **Node** tool, and then click and drag the node to the new position.

> 💡 When painting with the **Paintbrush**, you can temporarily switch to the **Node** tool by holding down the **Ctrl** key. This allows you to edit the nodes and control handles of your strokes as you go. To continue painting, simply release the **Ctrl** key.

To draw and edit brush strokes using a pen and tablet

- To create a brush stroke, use the pen and tablet exactly as you would use a 'real' pen or paintbrush on paper or canvas. Press down on the tablet where you want the stroke to start, and hold it down as you paint. The stroke appears immediately and follows your pen movements.

- To end the brush stroke, simply lift the pen off the tablet.

- To extend the brush stroke, position the pen cursor over one of the end nodes. The cursor changes to include a plus symbol. Press down on the node and drag the pen to add a brush stroke segment.

> 💡 For instructions on adjusting the **pressure sensitivity** of your Serif GraphicsPad pen and tablet, see the "Turn Photos into Art" Drawing Project.
>
> If you need help with installation, or other customization issues, see the *Serif GraphicsPad User Manual*.

- To redraw any part of the brush stroke, press and hold the **Ctrl** key and then click on a node and drag the stroke segment to the new position.

- Use the accompanying **Brush context toolbar** and **Pressure** tab to customize your brush strokes as you create them, as well as to edit brush strokes that you have already created. We'll discuss this in the following sections.

> 💡 To move a **group of nodes** on a brush stroke segment:
> - Click the ⟨⟩ **Node** tool and draw a selection box around the nodes you want to move.
> - Click and drag one of the selected nodes to move the whole group.

Use the Natural Media Brushes

The Brush context toolbar

When you create a brush stroke with the **Paintbrush** tool, the **Brush context toolbar** displays a selection of controls that you can use to adjust the appearance of the stroke.

Brush

This box displays the swatch for the brush style you select on the **Brushes** tab. Clicking the box opens the **Brush Edit** dialog, which you can use to make changes to a brush stroke. For example, you can adjust the size of the **Head**, **Body**, and **Tail** sections, or change the method used to repeat the body section. (Editing brush strokes is beyond the scope of this tutorial. For more information, see online Help or the "Make Your Own Brushes" tutorial.)

Colour

Clicking this button opens the **Colour Selector** dialog. Here you can edit the colour of your brush stroke.

For more information on defining and editing colours, see the online Help.

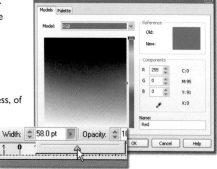

Width

This box displays the width, or thickness, of a brush stroke. To adjust the thickness, click the Up and Down arrows, or click the arrow to the right of the value box and then drag the slider.

Opacity

This box displays the opacity of a brush stroke. To adjust opacity, click the Up and Down arrows or click and drag the slider.

Our example shows the same stroke with 100%, 50%, and 25% opacity.

Smoothness

This box displays the smoothness of a brush stroke. To make a brush stroke more or less smooth, click the Up and Down arrows or click and drag the slider.

Select-on-Create

- If this button is **selected**, when you release the mouse button or take your pen off the tablet, the brush stroke you just created is automatically selected, allowing you to easily add to or edit it.

- If this button is **not selected**, when you release the mouse button or take your pen off the tablet, the brush stroke you just created is not selected. If you want to edit or add to the brush stroke, you must first click on it with the **Paintbrush** or **Node** tool.

Use the Natural Media Brushes

Fill-on-Create
Select this button if you want to fill shapes and curves
as you create them with your brush.

Example 1
Brush Style: Medium Paint 4
Width: 37
Opacity: 100%
Smoothness: 85%

Example 2
Brush Style: Medium Paint 4
Width: 56
Opacity: 100%
Smoothness: 85%

Example 3
Brush Style: Medium Paint 4
Width: 37
Opacity: 100%
Smoothness: 20%

Example 4
Brush Style: Medium Paint 4
Width: 37
Opacity: 50%
Smoothness: 20%

When you have created a brush stroke, you can select and edit it as just you would any other object
on your page.

Similarly, when you select a brush stroke, the controls that display on the context toolbar will change
depending on the particular tool you are using.

For example, try selecting a brush stroke with the **✐ Paintbrush** tool, the **➤ Pointer** tool, and the
▷ Node tool—as you switch from one tool to the next, you'll see a different set of controls displayed in
the context toolbar.

Use the Natural Media Brushes

The Pressure tab

When you work with paint, pencil, charcoal, or any other type of natural medium, you can dramatically change the appearance of your strokes by varying the pressure with which you apply the medium to the paper or canvas.

With DrawPlus, you can achieve the same flexibility in the following ways:

- By using a pressure-sensitive pen and tablet and varying pressure just as you would with a 'real' pencil or pen.

- By using the **Pressure** tab to adjust the pressure of strokes made with a pen and tablet and with a mouse. Note that you can also use this method to change the pressure of **previously created** strokes.

To see how you can control pressure-sensitivity using the **Pressure** tab, follow the procedure outlined below.

To adjust pressure-sensitivity

1 Click the ✏ **Paintbrush** tool, then on the **Brushes** tab select a stroke style of your choice and draw a line on the page.

2 With the brush stroke selected, click the **Pressure** tab (you may need to expand it—click the ▷ **Pressure Tab Menu** and then click **Expand**).

By default, this new brush stroke will have no pressure profile selected.

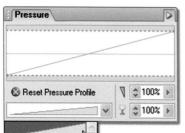

3 Click to expand the Pressure Profile drop-down list, and then click to select the first profile in the list.

The appearance of your brush stroke changes to reflect the new profile.

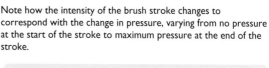

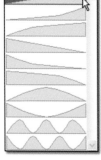

Note how the intensity of the brush stroke changes to correspond with the change in pressure, varying from no pressure at the start of the stroke to maximum pressure at the end of the stroke.

> 📍 When working with a pen and pressure-sensitive tablet, you can only apply a pressure profile to strokes you have previously created. By default, as you create a new stroke, pressure applied with the pen will override the pressure profile set on the **Pressure** tab.

Use the Natural Media Brushes

4 In the Pressure Profile drop-down list, select some different profiles and note how they affect the appearance of your brush stroke.

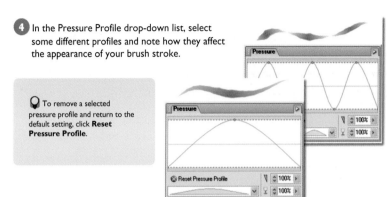

> 💡 To remove a selected pressure profile and return to the default setting, click **Reset Pressure Profile**.

As you can see, DrawPlus provides you with a range of preset pressure profiles from which to choose. However, you can also edit a profile and, if you wish, save it for use in future documents. Let's see how this is done...

To edit and save a new pressure profile

1 On the **Pressure** tab, choose any preset pressure profile from the list.

2 In the profile display pane, click a point on the blue profile line and drag to a new position.

A node is created at the new point—you can create as many of these nodes as you wish. After creating the nodes, you can move them or delete them as required:

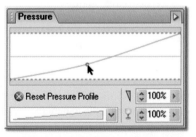

- To move a node, simply click and drag it.

- To delete a node, select it and then press **Delete**.

3 When you are happy with your pressure profile, click the 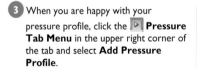 **Pressure Tab Menu** in the upper right corner of the tab and select **Add Pressure Profile**.

Your new profile is added to the preset pressure profiles in the drop-down list.

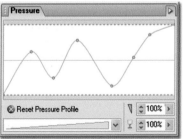

Use the Natural Media Brushes

Adjusting pressure variance

The dotted lines at the upper and lower edges of the profile display pane indicate the **range of variance** of the pressure profile. You can move these lines to limit the **maximum** and **minimum** pressure you want to apply with a brush stroke.

💡 This feature is particularly useful if you are using a mouse, since the mouse does not have the pressure-sensitivity of a pen and tablet.

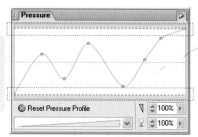

Example 1

Here, the maximum and minimum pressure values have not been adjusted, so the brush stroke pressure range is not limited.

Example 2

In this example, we **decreased the maximum pressure** value of the stroke by moving the upper line down.

Compared to Example 1, this brush stroke appears much less intense at its 'peak' points.

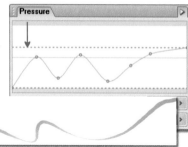

Example 3

Here we **increased the minimum pressure** value of the stroke by moving the lower line up.

Compared to Example 1, this brush stroke appears more intense at its 'trough' points.

As you can see, even if you do not have access to a pressure-sensitive pen and tablet, you can still produce realistic pressure variance with a mouse by simply adjusting the pressure profile of your brush strokes.

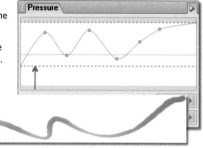

Use the Natural Media Brushes

Adjusting brush stroke thickness and transparency

Now let's look at the two controls in the lower right corner of the **Pressure** tab: **Thickness** and **Transparency**. Displayed as percentages, these values affect how the width and transparency of a brush stroke change as its pressure changes.

For example, suppose you are painting with a 'real' paintbrush... As you apply more pressure with the brush, the mark you make on the page becomes thicker and more dense (opaque). With DrawPlus, you can achieve the same effect. However, you can also limit how much the thickness and transparency will vary along the length of a particular brush stroke by adjusting these percentage values.

If you're having difficulty imagining this, the following examples should help.

Example 1

Thickness: 100%

Transparency: 100%

Here, we are allowing the maximum amount of variance along the length of the stroke.

As the stroke pressure decreases, note how the thickness decreases and the transparency increases correspondingly.

Example 2

Thickness: 0%

Transparency: 100%

We are allowing maximum variance for transparency, but no variance for thickness.

As the pressure decreases, the stroke becomes more transparent but the width of the stroke remains constant.

Example 3

Thickness: 100%

Transparency: 0%

We are allowing maximum variance for thickness, but no variance for transparency.

As the pressure decreases, the stroke becomes thinner but the transparency does not change.

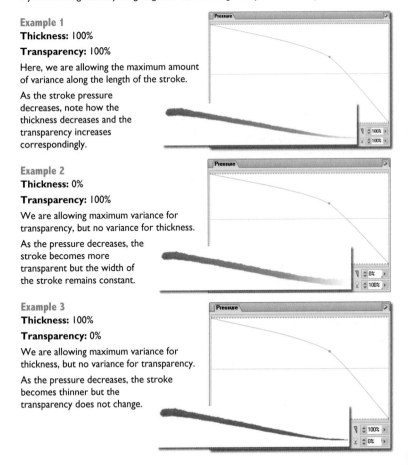

Use the Natural Media Brushes

Example 4
Thickness: 0%

Transparency: 0%

We are allowing no variance for thickness or transparency .

As the pressure decreases, there is no change in either the width or transparency of the brush stroke.

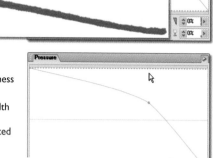

Example 5
Thickness: 50%

Transparency: 50%

We are allowing 50% variance for thickness and transparency.

As the pressure decreases, both the width and transparency of the brush stroke change. However, because we have limited the range of variance to 50% of the maximum, the end of the brush stroke is thicker and less transparent than in Example 1.

We suggest that you experiment with these settings yourself to see the different effects you can achieve.

Setting the default brush stroke

When you create any new object in DrawPlus, its appearance depends on the current **default settings** for the particular type of object.

Properties for brush strokes include width, colour, opacity, and smoothness. The term **default brush stroke** refers to the properties of the brush stroke that will be applied to the next new brush stroke you create.

> To view the current defaults for a particular object type, simply create a new object of that type. For more information, see online Help.

DrawPlus provides you with two methods of setting brush stroke (or any object) defaults:

- Update Defaults

- Synchronize Defaults

Updating defaults

Use this command to set up defaults before you create a new brush stroke.

To update brush stroke defaults

1 Create a single brush stroke and fine-tune its properties as desired—or use an existing brush stroke that already has the properties you want to use as the basis for new defaults.

2 Select the brush stroke, then right-click and select **Update Defaults** (or choose **Update Object Defaults** from the **Format** menu).

> Some default settings are recorded as 'master settings,' which will be in effect the next time you start DrawPlus or create a new document. You can change which settings become master settings. For details "Recording master settings" in online Help.

Synchronizing Defaults

On the Standard toolbar the  **Synchronize Defaults** drop-down list provides three options that you can use to control the default properties of any DrawPlus object. In this section, we'll discuss how these options specifically relate to brush strokes.

Synchronize Defaults

- If this option is **selected**, any new brush stroke you make (or any object you create—a line or Quick Shape for example) will assume the properties of the last stroke you created. If you change the properties again, those properties now become the new defaults and will be picked up by your next brush stroke.

  In addition, if you select (click on) a previously created brush stroke, your next stroke assumes the properties of the stroke you selected.

- If this option is **not selected**, any new brush stroke you make assumes the DrawPlus default properties. This means that if you want to continue painting with the same brush style settings, you have to reset the properties again for each new stroke.

Synchronization Settings

- Click this option to open the **Synchronize Defaults** dialog. Here, you can select which object attributes you want to become the new default properties. Any new brush stroke will now assume only the *selected properties* of the last stroke you created. If you change the properties again, those properties will be picked up by the next stroke.

  If you select a previously created brush stroke, your next stroke assumes the properties of the stroke you selected.

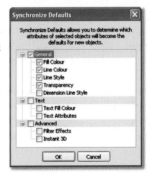

Use the Natural Media Brushes

Reset Object Defaults

- If you click this option, DrawPlus will revert to the original **global** defaults. This means that if you've changed defaults for other objects, such as shapes and lines, those defaults will also be reverted.

    Note: To reset object defaults for the **current object** only, click the 🖉 **Reset Current Object Defaults** button.

To create brush strokes without synchronizing defaults

1 In the **Synchronize Defaults** drop-down list, clear the **Synchronize Defaults** option, and then create a few black brush strokes on your page.

2 Use the 🖈 **Pointer** tool to select one of the strokes, then on the **Swatches** tab, change the stroke colour to red.

3 Click the 🖉 **Paintbrush** tool and paint a new stroke. The colour reverts to the black of your original stroke.

To synchronize brush stroke defaults

1 In the **Synchronize Defaults** drop-down list, click **Synchronization Settings**. In the dialog, in the **General** section, click the following properties: **Fill Colour, Line Colour, Line Style,** and **Transparency.**

    Now create a few black brush strokes on your page.

2 Use the 🖈 **Pointer** tool to select a stroke, then on the **Swatches** tab, change the stroke colour to red.

3 Click the 🖉 **Paintbrush** tool again and paint a new brush stroke. The new stroke picks up the red colour of the previous stroke.

4 Create a new stroke and apply a different colour.

5 Create another stroke—the stroke picks up the colour you chose in step 4.

6 Using the **Paintbrush** tool, click on one of the red brush strokes and then draw a new stroke.

    This stroke picks up the defaults from the stroke you just clicked, so it will be red.

Congratulations, you've completed the tutorial! As you can see, there's a lot you can do with the media brushes. (You'll find more information in Chapter 5 of the *DrawPlus User Guide* and in online Help.)

We hope that you're feeling a little more comfortable using these powerful tools and are looking forward to creating your own natural media masterpieces.

Create Filter Effects

Transform a standard smiley into an impressive contoured creation with filter effects.

In this exercise, you'll learn how to:

- Create a new document.

- Work with Quick Shapes.

- Align objects on a page.

- Combine objects.

- Add bevel and emboss and lighting filter effects.

- Convert an object into a keyframe animation.

- Export an animation to a video file.

Create Filter Effects

1 In the DrawPlus Startup Wizard, choose **Drawing**. Select a page size of your choice and click **Open**.

2 On the left Drawing toolbar, on the Quick Shapes flyout, click the **Quick Face**. Press and hold the **Ctrl** key (to constrain the shape to a circle), and then draw a face near the centre of your page. (We suggest you make the diameter of the face about 10 cm.)

3 On the **Swatches** tab, click a bright yellow swatch.

4 On the **Line** tab, remove the outline by setting the line style to **None**.

5 Now click the **Quick Ellipse** and draw a circle the same size as the **Quick Face**. If you need to, you can set exact values by typing them directly into the **W** and **H** boxes on the **Transform** tab.

> 💡 To display or hide the various DrawPlus tabs, click on the arrow in the upper right corner of any tab, then click **Studio tabs**.

6 Set the circle colour to bright blue and remove the outline.

7 Press **Ctrl+A** to select both objects.

8 On the **Align** tab, select the **Include Page** check box and then click 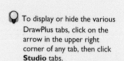 **Vertical Centre** and 🔲 **Horizontal Centre** to centre the objects on the page.

> 💡 You can also use the **Align** tab or the **Arrange** menu to align objects on your page.

9 Click off to one side to deselect the items, then click on them until the HintLine tells you that the **Quick Face** is selected. Right-click and choose **Copy** to copy this object to the Clipboard—we'll need it shortly.

10 Click and drag a rectangular selection box around both items to select them, then click the 🔲 **Combine** button.

The shapes reform into a new shape called a '**polycurve.**'

11 Select the new shape, then on the Drawing toolbar, click *fx* **Filter Effects**.

12 In the **Filter Effects** dialog, in the **Effects** list on the left, select the **Bevel and Emboss** check box. Set the **Blur** to 30 and the **Depth** to 600. Click **OK**.

13 On the **Edit** menu, click **Paste** (or press **Ctrl+V**) to paste the copied **Quick Face** into your drawing. Set the fill colour to bright blue.

14 Select the **Quick Face** and click *fx* **Filter Effects**.

15 In the **Filter Effects** dialog, select the **Bevel and Emboss** check box. In the **Bevel and Emboss** section, in the **Style** drop-down list, select 'Inner Bevel.' Set the **Blur** to 10 and the **Depth** to 500. Click **OK**.

16 Repeat steps 7 and 8 to align the items in the centre of the page.

In the following section, we'll make use of the new DrawPlus X2 keyframe animation functionality to make the face appear to rotate.

To transform the image into a rotating animation

1 On the **File** menu, choose **Convert to Keyframe Animation**.

At the bottom of the workspace, click the ▬▬ **Open/Close** button to display the **Storyboard** tab. You'll see your first keyframe displayed.

2 On the **Storyboard** tab, click ▣ **Insert**. In the **Insert Keyframe** dialog, extend the animation by 5 seconds and click **OK**. A new blank keyframe is created and displayed on the **Storyboard** tab.

3 In the first keyframe, select everything on the page. To the lower right of the image, click ▶▶ **Run Forward**.

4 In the **Run Forward** dialog, in the **Run Length** drop-down list, select **To end of storyboard** and click **OK**.

A second keyframe is added to the **Storyboard** tab.

5 In the new keyframe, select everything on the page and click *fx* **Filter Effects**.

6 In the **Filter Effects** dialog, adjust the **Angle** (of the light source) of the **Bevel and Emboss** effect to 359.

Create Filter Effects

7 To preview the animation, click **File** and then click **Preview in Browser**.

Your animation will play to the end and then start again—a process called looping. By default, keyframe animations will loop continuously. However, suppose we want this animation to play once and then stop. We can easily do this by using a **marker**.

8 On the **Storyboard** tab, to the right of keyframe 2, click the marker arrowhead.

9 In the **Marker** dialog, type a name for the marker, select the **Stops playhead** option, and then click **OK**.

10 Preview your animation again—it should play once and then stop.

You can now proceed to the next section and export your animation to video.

To export your animation to video

1 On the **File**, menu, click then **Export**, then **Export as Video**.

2 In the **Keyframe Animation Video Export** dialog, on the **Basic** tab:

- In the **Filename** box, type a name for your video.

- Click the **Browse** button, browse to locate your save location and click **Save**.

- In the **File** type drop-down list, choose your preferred output file type.

- In the **Template** drop-down list, select an Internet connection speed.

- In the **Quality** drop-down list, select your preferred output file quality.

> Your **Template** and **Quality** choices will depend on the intended audience of your video. For example, if you intend to share your animation on a Web site, think about the connection speed that best suits your audience. The templates are listed in the order of low- to high-speed connections, giving increasing levels of video quality.

3 Click **Export**.

When the export has completed, the **Export Complete** dialog opens.

4 To view your video file:

- To open the file in the default media player, click **Open**.

- or -

- To open the folder containing the video file, click **Open Folder**. Simply double-click on the file to open it in the default media player.

You can also export keyframe animations to Flash SWF file format. For details, see online Help.

Create 3D Effects

DrawPlus X2 provides the **Instant 3D** tool, which applies a 3D effect and then allows 'in-place' editing of your 3D object.

In this exercise, you will:

- Create and format artistic text.

- Change font style, size, and colour.

- Apply an Instant 3D effect.

- Adjust 3D settings to obtain different effects.

- Apply a bitmap fill.

Create 3D Effects

1 In the DrawPlus Startup Wizard, choose **Drawing**, select a page size of your choice and click **Open**.

2 On the left Drawing toolbar, click the **Λ Artistic Text** tool. Click and drag on your page to create a large text insertion point and then type some text.

3D FX

3 Triple-click to select the entire text object, then on the Text context toolbar, change the point size of the text to 160 and choose a chunky bold font style.

3D FX

4 On the **Colour** or **Swatches** tab, select a solid fill—we've chosen orange because it will show up the bevels we are going to add later.

5 Click the **⬉ Pointer** tool, then click and drag the object into position it just inside the page margins.

> 💡 A chunky bold font works well for this effect. We've used **Basic Sans Heavy SF**.
>
> If you don't already have this font installed, you can install it from the DrawPlus Program CD-ROM.

6 Select your text object and then on the Drawing toolbar, click **📀 Instant 3D**.

The text adopts 3D characteristics and a blue orbit circle is displayed in the foreground. This circle allows you to rotate the object around the X-, Y-, and Z- axes.

7 Click and drag at various points around the circle. As you move over the nodes, notice that the cursor changes to denote the orientation of the rotation.

8 On the Instant 3D context toolbar, in the 3D Effects category drop-down list, choose **Bevel**. (The toolbar options change dynamically according to the category currently selected.)

- In the Bevel Profile drop-down list, select the third profile and click **✔ OK**.

- Set a **Depth** value of 0.2 cm; an **Inner** value of 0.15 cm, and an **Outer** value of 0.04 cm

9 In the 3D Effects category drop-down list, choose **Lights**. This setting is used to adjust the amount and direction of lighting that produces the 3D effect.

- Set the **Angle** to 350 and the **Elevation** to 70.

Create 3D Effects

10 In the 3D Effects category drop-down list, choose **Lathe**.

- Set the **Extrusion** value to 1.45 cm and the **Outer** value to 0.04 cm.

11 In the 3D Effects category drop-down list, choose **Viewport**.

- Set the **Lens** to 45; the **X** rotation to 20; the **Y** rotation to 30; and the **Z** rotation to 16.

12 In the 3D Effects category drop-down list, choose **Material**.

- Set the **Base** to 71% and the **Highlight** to 93%.

Your text object should resemble our illustration on the right.

Now let's see how Instant 3D works with bitmap fills.

13 On the **Swatches** tab, in the 🎴▾ **Bitmap** drop-down list, select the 'Wood' subcategory.

Click the 'wood02' bitmap fill, drag it over to your text object, and then release the mouse button.

14 Return to the Instant 3D context toolbar. In the 3D Effects category drop-down list, choose **Texture**.

- In the **Projection** drop-down list, select **Side**.

The wrap now extends around the sides of the extruded text object.

💡 To edit base properties of a selected 3D object, use the ▷ **Node** tool. The object is shown without its 3D effect, allowing its selection handles and nodes to be manipulated.

If you want to experiment further, you can modify the colours, try some three- and four-colour fills, and adjust the Instant 3D settings to further customize the object.

Work With Line Tools

Learn how to use the **Pen** and **Node** tools to best advantage.

In this exercise, you will:

- Import an image file.

- Adjust the transparency of an image.

- Trace around an object using the **Pen** tool.

- Adjust curves using nodes and control handles.

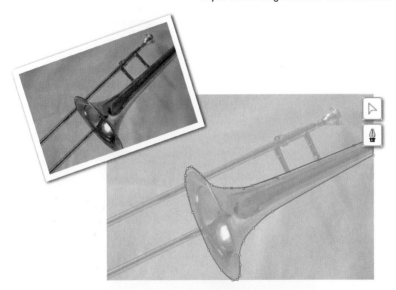

Work With Line Tools

In this tutorial, we'll be tracing around an object with varied curves, using an imported photo of a trombone.

1 In the DrawPlus Startup Wizard, choose **Drawing**. Select a page size of your choice and click **Open**.

2 On the Drawing toolbar, click 🖼 **Insert Picture**. In the **Insert Picture** dialog, browse to locate the **Trombone.jpg** file in your **Workspace** folder.

In a typical default installation, you'll find this in the following location:

C:\Program Files\Serif\DrawPlus\X2\Tutorials\Workspace

Click on the **Trombone.jpg** file, and then click **Open**.

3 Click on your page to place the photo at actual size.

On the HintLine toolbar, click ⊕ **Zoom In** or drag the Zoom slider to zoom into the image.

💡 You can make the image easier to trace around by applying transparency. To do this, select the image and then on the **Transparency** tab click the 50% swatch.

4 On the Drawing toolbar, click the ✒ **Pen** tool.

At the left of the Pen context toolbar, notice that the **Pen** tool has two creation modes:

- ⌒ **Smooth joins**

- ⌃ **Sharp joins**

These options let you create smooth curve or sharp 'cusp' points as you lay down the nodes that make up your curve. As our image is predominantly comprised of curves, we'll work in **Smooth joins** creation mode.

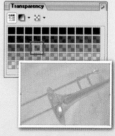

5 On the context toolbar, click ⌒ **Smooth joins**.

6 Click at the top right of the trombone, then continue clicking to place 'nodes' around the outline.

(You don't have to be exact; we'll tidy up later.)

Work With Line Tools

The illustration below shows the order of the places we clicked to trace the outline of the trombone in an anti-clockwise direction.

You can make the shape as complicated or as simple as you wish.

This tutorial steers a middle course—but it can be done with fewer or more nodes.

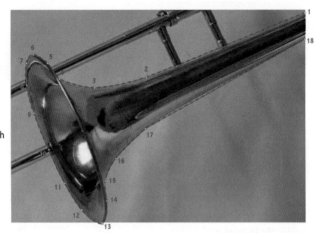

⑦ When you reach the last node (18 in our example), close the shape.

To do this, on the Text context toolbar, click ⊦•⊦ **Close Curve**.

When you have completed your outline, you will probably find that some areas of your curve need to be adjusted.

We'll do this next by adjusting nodes, curve segments, and control handles.

⑧ On the Drawing toolbar, click the ▷ **Node** tool, or with the **Pen** tool still selected, hold down the **Ctrl** key to switch temporarily to the **Node** tool.

There are various ways to reshape your outline using this tool:

• To shape a curve using a node, simply click and drag it (Figure 1).

• To shape a curve using a control (Bézier) handle, click and drag the handle ends (Figure 2).

Figure 1   **Figure 2**

Work With Line Tools

- To shape a curve segment (the portion of a curve between two nodes), click on the curve segment and drag it (Figure 3).

- To add a node, click at the point where you want to add the node (Figure 4).

Figure 3   **Figure 4**

Experiment with these techniques to fine-tune your outline.

Before we end this tutorial, let's look at another way to use nodes to shape a curve.

Node types

As we've just seen, curves consist of curve segments, nodes and control handles. When you click on a node, the **node type** buttons become available for selection from the context toolbar. The behaviour of the control handles, and the curvature of the segments on either side of a node, depend on whether the node is sharp, smooth, symmetric, or smart.

- **Sharp Corner:** Curve segments either side of the node are completely independent.

- **Smooth Corner:** The slope of the curve is the same on both sides of the node (the depth of the two joined segments can be different).

- **Symmetric Corner:** Nodes join curve segments with the same slope and depth on both sides of the node.

- **Smart Corner:** Nodes automatically determine slope and depth for a rounded, best-fitting curve.

> When you click to place a node, as we did in this exercise, the default node type is **Smart Corner** (when you edit its control handles, both sides of the curve at that point will react in the same way).
>
> When you click and drag to place a node, the default node type is **Smooth Corner**.

(See 'Changing nodes and line segments' in the 'Editing lines and shapes' online Help topic.)

To change node type

1 Click the ▷ **Node** tool, select the object and then select the node you want to change (**Shift**-click to select multiple nodes).

2 On the context toolbar, click the node type you want to switch to.

To see how these node types behave, create a new curve, hold down the **Ctrl** key and select a node, and then switch between the various node types. In some cases, the curve will change as soon as the new node type is clicked, in other cases, you'll need to drag the control handles to see how the behaviour changes.

What you do with your outlined shapes is entirely up to you. Try modifying the colours, adding colour fills, or applying 3D effects to customize the objects.

> If you adjust the control handles of a **Smart Corner** node, it switches to a **Smooth Corner**. You can reset the node type on the context toolbar—but if you want to maintain your smart corners, be careful what you click and drag!

Create a Velvet Effect

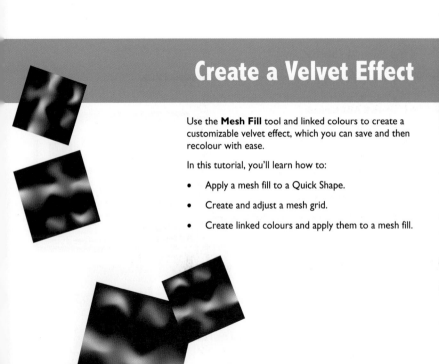

Use the **Mesh Fill** tool and linked colours to create a customizable velvet effect, which you can save and then recolour with ease.

In this tutorial, you'll learn how to:

- Apply a mesh fill to a Quick Shape.

- Create and adjust a mesh grid.

- Create linked colours and apply them to a mesh fill.

Create a Velvet Effect

1 In the DrawPlus Startup Wizard, choose **Drawing**, select a page size of your choice and click **Open**.

2 On the Quick Shape flyout, click the ☐ **Quick Rectangle**, then hold down the **Ctrl** key and draw a large square out to the page edge.

> 💡 Hold down the **Ctrl** key to maintain the aspect ratio of the shape you are drawing.

Before we apply colour to our shape, let's first create a **linked colour**. You'll see the benefits of this later...

3 On the **Swatches** tab:

- In the 🎨 ▾ **Palettes** drop-down list, click **Standard RGB**.

- Right-click anywhere on the palette and then click **Add Linked**.

4 In the **Colour Selector** dialog:

- In the **R**, **G**, and **B** boxes, type the values 64, 0, and 64 respectively.

- In the **Name** box, type a name for your linked colour. Click **OK**.

A swatch of your linked colour displays at the bottom of the **Swatches** tab.

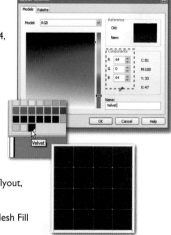

5 Click the ↖ **Pointer** tool and then select your square. On the **Swatches** tab click to fill the shape withy your linked colour.

6 On the Drawing toolbar, on the ◈ ◈ **Fill** tool flyout, click the ◈ **Mesh Fill** tool.

A 4 by 4 grid is applied to your shape and the Mesh Fill context toolbar displays.

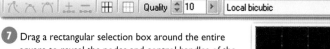

7 Drag a rectangular selection box around the entire square to reveal the nodes and control handles of the mesh.

We'll now add more colour nodes to this fill.

Don't worry if you don't add the nodes in the right place—with a single click on the Mesh Fill context toolbar we can force the nodes to form a regular grid before we proceed.

Mesh Fill context toolbar

Displays curve editing functions for working with mesh fills. The nodes in a mesh fill plot areas of colour; the curve handles attached to each node dictate how far the influence of that node's colour will stretch and in what direction. Generally, nodes have short perpendicular curve handles but you may need to make sharp nodes so that they have different colour stretching on different sides of the node. Symmetrical curve handles make nodes apply an even colour influence around the node. You'll find the following options on the toolbar:

Make node sharp

Make node smooth   For more information, see the DrawPlus online Help.

Make node symmetrical

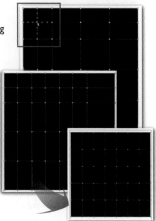

8 Double-click in the middle of the first square of the grid. A new node appears, with two lines intersecting it—one vertical and one horizontal.

9 Repeat the previous step inside the next two squares of the top row of the grid, (leaving the rightmost square as it is) to create a 7 by 5 uneven grid.

10 On the Mesh Fill context toolbar, click ⊞ **Reset Mesh** to create a regular grid of nodes.

We can now start to apply various shades of purple to the nodes of the grid.

11 Click off the mesh grid to deselect all the nodes. Now drag a rectangular selection box around just the upper two nodes on the third vertical line inside the shape.

12 On the **Colour** tab, in the drop-down list, click **Tinting**.

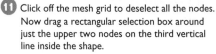

13 Apply a lighter purple tint to the nodes by clicking a point in the large tint swatch, or by clicking and dragging the slider.

Note that the **Colour** values update as you click on different area of the swatch.

Create a Velvet Effect

14 Click on any *single* node inside the grid.

On the **Colour** tab click to apply a colour tint to the node.

15 Drag a rectangular selection box around any *group* of nodes inside the grid.

On the **Colour** tab click to apply a colour tint to the selected nodes.

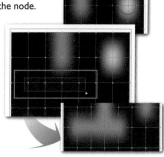

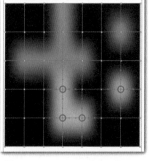

16 Hold down the **Shift** key, and this time click to select a few random nodes.

On the **Colour** tab click to apply a colour tint to the selected nodes.

17 Use the methods described above to apply varying shades of purple to random nodes and groups of nodes in the mesh grid.

Now we'll deform the grid by moving nodes. We can then save the fill we've created for future use.

The next steps will take a few minutes, with no particular right or wrong result.

18 Click to select the first node in the upper right corner of the inside of the shape.

Drag the node down and slightly to the right.

You can also try dragging the node's curve handles to adjust the effect.

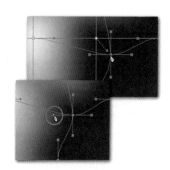

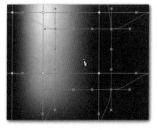

19 Click inside one of the squares to add a red 'target.' Notice that this selects the surrounding group of nodes and control handles. Drag the target to reposition the selected node group.

20 Repeat the process until you've achieved an effect you are happy with.

21 To see what your velvet effect looks like without the mesh grid, press the **Esc** key to remove the grid.

If you want to go back and edit the effect, click the 🖎 **Mesh Fill** tool to redisplay the grid.

When you're happy with your adjusted nodes and the velvet effect produced, you can save it for use in future DrawPlus documents.

To save the fill to the Swatches tab

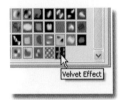

1 Right-click your object, click **Add to Studio**, then click **Fill**.

2 In the **Add Fill to Gallery** dialog, name your design and click **OK**.

Your custom fill is saved to the **Swatches** tab.

To save the fill to the Gallery tab

1 On the **Gallery** tab, in the category drop-down list, select **My Designs**.

2 Select the ⬉ **Pointer** tool, click on your filled object, then drag it over to the **Gallery** tab.

3 In the **Add Design** dialog, name your design and click **OK**.

A swatch of your design is added to the **Gallery** tab.

As a final touch, we'll show you how to change the colour of your velvet square by changing the base colour of the mesh fill.

In the following simple procedure, you'll see why we used a linked colour for our velvet design.

To change a linked colour

1 On the **Swatches** tab, right-click the purple linked colour swatch you created for your velvet effect, and click **Edit**.

2 In the **Colour Selector** dialog, to choose a new base colour for your velvet square:

Create a Velvet Effect

- Click a point in the large colour square.

- or -

- Drag the slider on the colour bar.

- or -

- Type values into the **R**, **G**, and **B** boxes.

Click **OK**.

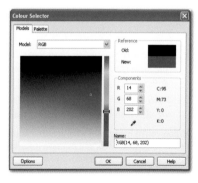

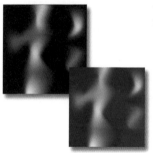

With this single click, the base colour and its various tints all update to create a new square of velvet in your chosen colour!

Now that you've gone to the trouble of creating a custom mesh fill effect, and understand the concept of linked colours, take advantage of these exciting DrawPlus features in your future creations.

Draw a Flow Chart

Should you take the train to work, or drive? Perhaps a simple flow chart will aid in resolving this profound question—and help you understand connecting lines at the same time.

In this tutorial, you'll learn how to:

- Set the properties of connecting lines.
- Use **Quick Rectangles** and lines to draw a flow chart.
- Work with connector tools.
- Align and rearrange flow chart elements.

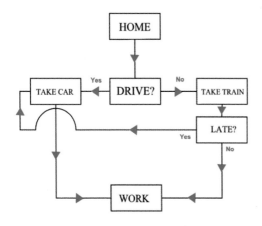

Draw a Flow Chart

1 In the DrawPlus Startup Wizard, choose **Drawing**, select a page size of your choice and click **Open**.

Before proceeding, let's set the following properties for connecting lines:

- **Bridge Radius**—the size of the bridge which jumps over other connecting lines.

- **Bridge Gap**—the distance between two adjacent bridges.

- **Standoff**—the minimum clearance between a connector and any adjacent object.

2 On the **Tools** menu, click **Options**.

3 In the **Options** dialog, click the **Layout** option.

For this example we're going to create fairly large 'auto connectors.'

4 Set the **Ruler Units** to millimetres. Set both the **Bridge Radius** and **Bridge Gap** to 10 mm; set the **Standoff** value to 5 mm. Click **OK**.

To begin, we'll draw the necessary flow chart boxes.

We could create a draft layout on paper first, and then recreate the layout in DrawPlus. However, the advantage of designing directly on screen is that if you decide to move the boxes, the connectors will automatically redraw to the new position.

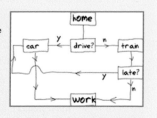

5 On the Quick Shapes flyout, select a **Quick Rectangle** and draw a rectangle about 25 mm wide by 12 mm deep.

6 Drag this shape to the 'Home' position in the layout, as illustrated in our pencil illustration above.

7 Right-click on the box and choose **Connectors**. If the **Obstructive Object** property is not already checked, click to select it.

This ensures that any connecting lines will treat the box as an obstacle and route around it.

8 Duplicate the first box five times. To do this:

- Click on the object, hold down the **Ctrl** key, and then drag to a new position on the page.

-or-

- Right-click the object and click **Copy**. Right-click again and click **Paste**. Repeat to create a total of six boxes.

We'll now link the boxes.

> To precisely position your boxes and connectors later, use the **Align** tab or right-click on the objects and click **Align Objects**.

9 On the Drawing toolbar, on the Lines flyout, click the 🔧 **Connector** tool. The following specialized tools are now available on the Context toolbar:

🔧 **Direct Connector**—to create straight or diagonal line between points.

🔧 **Right Angle Connector**—to create "dog-leg" connection between points.

🔧 **Auto Connector**—which decides on the best course.

✳ **Connection Point**—which enables you to add your own points.

For this exercise we'll use the **Auto Connector** tool since this automatically forms bridges. (If no lines cross, you could use Direct and Right Angle Connectors.)

10 On the Context toolbar, click the **Auto Connector** tool.

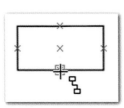

11 Hover the cursor over the boxes on your page—default connection points appear as red crosses the sides of the shape. When you move the mouse over any connection point, a blue box appears around it; you can then drag to connect this point to any other.

12 Try this by clicking on the lower cross of the top box, and dragging to the upper cross of the box below.

13 Your first line should now be linking the top two boxes. Repeat this process using our pencil illustration as the template for all links except the one from 'Late' to 'Car.' This last one will require a **Bridge** connector.

14 To create a Bridge connector, drag from the left node of the 'Late' box to the left connector of the 'Car' box. The line should jump over the vertical line when you release the mouse button.

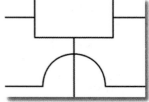

Draw a Flow Chart

In the finished chart, we've altered the shape of a couple of boxes, typed some text inside them (just select the shape and start typing), and placed some arrows to indicate the 'flow.'

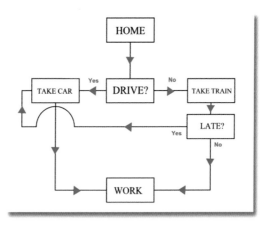

 If you create new elements like these arrows and the words 'Yes' and 'No,' make sure that their **Obstructive Object** property is not selected, otherwise your connecting lines will try to route around them. You could perhaps more easily add arrowheads to each connection line, using the **Line** tab—and try altering other line style properties while you're at it!

That's it, you've completed your flow chart. If you now want to rearrange your chart, just click on a box and move it. The links will follow!

This has been a simple example, but connectors will really prove their worth the next time you have a complex schedule or family tree to work out!

 On the **Gallery** tab, take a look at the **Connecting Symbols** category. Here you'll find an array of basic shapes and chart symbols you can use as starting points

You can even create your own family tree—see the "Make a Family Tree" Drawing Project.

Create Web Button Rollovers

When you point to a Web page graphic, your mouse pointer physically enters the screen region occupied by the graphic. You might click then on the graphic, or move the mouse out of the button region.

Underlying code can detect any of these mouse events and cause a new graphic to be swapped into the same region. In this way, a button graphic that normally appears 'up' might instantly change to 'down' when the mouse rolls over it.

In DrawPlus, it's easy to define multiple 'rollover states' for a Web graphic; the necessary JavaScript code is generated automatically. In this tutorial you'll see just how easy it can be.

In this exercise, you'll learn how to:

- Set up page dimensions and ruler units.

- Add filter effects to Quick Shapes.

- Create slice objects and set their properties.

- Preview your finished Web button in a Web browser.

- Export your Web button and its rollover states.

Create Web Button Rollovers

1 In the DrawPlus Startup Wizard, choose **Drawing**, select any page size of your choice and click **Open**.

Next we'll switch to pixel-based ruler units, and trim the page area.

2 On the **Tools** menu, click **Options**.

3 In the **Options** dialog, click the **Layout** option, set the **Ruler Units** to 'pixels' and click **OK**.

4 On the **File** menu, click **Page Setup**.

5 In the **Page Setup** dialog, in the **Document Size** section, set the **Width** to 760 and the **Height** to 420. Click **OK**.

Now we'll create a button.

6 On the left Drawing toolbar, on the Quick Shapes flyout, select the ☐ **Quick Rectangle**. Drag out a rectangle roughly 120 pixels wide by 40 high.

7 Drag the shape's slider to the top to create a round-edged lozenge shape.

8 On the **Swatches** tab, apply any solid colour fill.

9 On the **Line** tab, remove the outline from the shape by selecting **None** from the line style drop-down list.

10 On the Drawing toolbar, click *fx* **Filter Effects**.

11 In the **Filter Effects** dialog:

- In the **Effects** list, select **Bevel and Emboss**.

- In the **Style** box, select **Inner Bevel**.

- For the **Highlight**, select Normal, white, and 80% opacity.

- For the **Shadow,** select Normal, white, and 80% opacity.

- Set the **Blur** to 15, the **Depth** to 200, **Soften** to 0, **Angle** to 90, and **Elevation** to 45.

- Click **OK**.

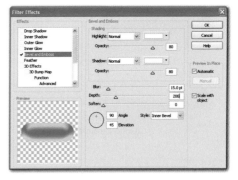

Create Web Button Rollovers

12 Click the ✸ **Pointer** tool, select the lozenge, then type some text inside the shape (this is **shape text**).

13 Format your text as desired. (You can't change the outline colour of shape text, so if you want to do this, you'll need to use the **Λ Artistic Text** tool to create **artistic text**.)

14 Right-click your newly created button and click **Insert Slice Object**. 'Slice lines' now display on your page, defining the button as a separate Web object.

15 Double-click the shaded interior region of your button to open the **Image Slice Object Properties** dialog.

16 In the **Rollover Details** section, click to select the **Over** and **Down** check boxes and click **OK**.

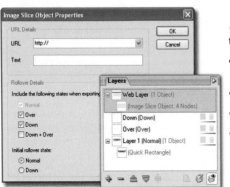

On the **Layers** tab, you'll now see four layers in the document:

- **Web Layer**—containing the image slice object
- **Down**
- **Over**
- **Normal**—containing the Quick Rectangle

ℹ️ The Image Slice Properties dialog

Use this dialog, to define the various states and actions that will be associated with a button when it's on a Web page. The **URL** box usually defines a hyperlink target page, and the **Text** box stores a popup 'tooltip' message displayed on a rollover event. In the **Rollover Details** section you can select how many button states you want to be active.

- **Normal**—this is the standard state of the graphic before any rollover, and is always included.
- **Over**—the state triggered by a mouseover.
- **Down**—the state triggered by a mouse click on the graphic.
- **Down + Over** is rarely used.

Create Web Button Rollovers

We already have a graphic on our **Normal** layer, so all we need to do now is create a variant state (a different graphic) on the **Over** and **Down** layers—for the rollover states we intend to activate.

> ⓘ For future reference, note that slice objects can be moved, resized, and edited just like normal objects.

17 Select the button object, copy it from the **Normal** layer, then on the **Layers** tab, click the **Over** layer to switch to that layer.

18 Paste the copy on to the **Over** layer (the button will appear in precise alignment with the original). On the **Swatches** tab, apply a different fill colour.

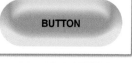

19 Click the **Down** layer tab, paste again, and apply another colour.

At this point you can preview your efforts in a Web browser.

20 On the **File** menu, click **Preview in Browser**. This launches your default browser and displays the button onscreen.

21 Roll your mouse over the button and click to see the variant 'Over' and 'Down' graphics you defined.

Create Web Button Rollovers

To export the button along with its defined rollover states

1 On the **Normal** layer, select the slice object and on the **File** menu, click **Export as Image**.

2 In the **Export Optimizer** dialog, on the **Format** tab, select an appropriate file type (typically JPG or GIF) and choose your settings.

3 On the **Settings** tab:

- Use a **dpi** of 96 (customary for onscreen graphics).

- Select the **Image Slices** check box.

- Click **Export**.

Congratulations, you've exported your Web button along with its rollover states!

DrawPlus creates a file for each image state, as well as a single file containing the HTML code that you can copy and paste into the <head> section of your Web page.

If you're creating Web images, you'll also want to explore the **Web** toolbar. This toolbar is hidden by default.—to display it, on the **View** menu, click **Toolbars** and then select **Web Toolbar**. The toolbar displays on the left, below the **Drawing** toolbar.

In addition to the **Image Slice** tool, the Web toolbar provides the ☐ **Hotspot Rectangle,** ◯ **Hotspot Circle,** and ⬡ **Hotspot Polygon** tools. These tools let you create hotspots (linked regions) on specific portions of an image.

Rollover states don't work with hotspots, but you can draw and then edit the hotspots just like ordinary shapes to create irregular zones (like countries on a map, for example), each of which links to a separate page.

See the DrawPlus online Help for more details.

Create Metallic Text

Apply linear fills and other effects to create 'metallic' text.

This tutorial shows you how to:

- Create and format text objects.

- Use the **Fill** tool.

- Add colours to a basic linear fill.

- Create a custom linear fill and save it for future use.

Create Metallic Text

1 In the DrawPlus Startup Wizard, choose **Drawing**, select a page size of your choice and click **Open**.

2 On the left Drawing toolbar, select the Λ **Artistic Text** tool and draw the initial character at approximately 3.5 cm (1.5 in) tall. Type "Metallic" and on the **Text** context toolbar, set the font to Grenoble Heavy SF.

3 Click the **Fill** tool and draw a vertical line through your text.

We'll be adding colours to the basic linear fill just created so you may want to either draw the line longer than required (and redraw it afterwards) or zoom in so that the fill path is large enough to work along.

> 💡 If you hold down the **Shift** key while you draw, the fill will 'snap' the line in 15° increments.

4 With the **Fill** tool still selected, click the **Swatches** tab and then in the 🎨 ▾ **Palettes** drop-down list, select the **Standard RGB** palette.

5 On the palette, click a colour swatch—we used RGB (92, 188, 252)—and then drag it on to the top square node of the fill path.

Hover your mouse over the **Swatches** tab's colours to see their RGB values appear as Tooltips. We used the following six colours, but you can use any colours you prefer.

- RGB (92, 188, 252)
- RGB (186, 218, 255)
- RGB (250, 250, 250)
- RGB (203, 203, 203)
- RGB (135, 135, 135)
- RGB (128, 128, 255)

6 Drag the second (pale blue) colour over the dotted fill line, when the cursor changes to incorporate a + symbol, release the mouse button. This adds a node and a key colour to the gradient, using the selected colour.

7 Repeat this procedure with the remaining colours to create the chrome effect. You can move the nodes up and down the fill path to change how they blend together.

8 Once your fill contains the right colours in the right places, right-click it, choose **Add to Studio**, and then click **Fill**.

9 In the **Add Fill to Gallery** dialog, type an appropriate name for your custom fill and click **OK**.

DrawPlus appends the new fill to its existing set of Linear fills—so you can use it in other documents.

10 To view the thumbnail of your new fill:

On the **Swatches** tab, in the 🎨 ▾ **Gradient** drop-down list, click **Linear**.

11 Now create a separate piece of text that reads "SHEEN."

12 Make this text approximately 150 pt in size and apply a bold chunky font (we used Plakette 4 SF). Position the text below the word Metallic.

13 On the **Swatches** tab, in the 🎨 ▾ **Gradient** fill drop-down list, select **Plasma** and apply the **Plasma 2 fill**.

14 Use the 🔶 **Fill** tool to move the nodes on the outside of the fill, stretching and skewing the fill effect to better resemble a brushed metal finish.

15 You may want to save this fill for future use, too.

Once the effects are achieved, you can add perspective and rotate the objects—you could also try using filter effects to add bevels.

> 💡 The fonts used in this tutorial are included with DrawPlus.
>
> If you haven't installed these fonts, you can do so from the *DrawPlus Program CD-ROM*.

Create a Glass Effect

Create a glass effect for text using filter effects and transparency.

In this exercise, you'll learn how to:

- Create and format text objects.

- Work with fills and transparency.

- Apply filter effects.

Create a Glass Effect

1 In the DrawPlus Startup Wizard, choose **Drawing**, select a page size of your choice and click **Open**.

2 On the Drawing toolbar, click the Λ **Artistic Text** tool and create a text object to almost fill your page. We've typed the word "Glass."

> It's more effective if you use a chunky bold font for this effect.

3 Copy the text object (by selecting **Copy** from the **Edit** menu, or by pressing **Ctrl+C**), and then paste two copies directly on top of your original (by pressing **Ctrl+V** twice).

4 The top-most of the three text objects is selected by default. On the **Colour** tab, double-click the **Fill** button to open the **Colour Selector** dialog.

- On the **Models** tab, in the **Model** drop-down list, select **RGB**.

- In the **Components** section, set the object fill to a dark blue/green by entering RGB values of 0, 112, and 112 respectively.

5 On the **Transparency** tab, click the ▦ **Solid** button and apply a 10% solid opacity.

6 Click once on your stacked text objects to select the middle text object. Set the fill colour to medium grey and apply a 10% opacity.

7 Click once more on your text objects. This selects the bottom-most text object. Set the fill colour to white.

8 On the **Transparency** tab, in the ◰ ▾ **Gradient** drop-down list, select **Plasma** and apply the **Plasma 13** transparency.

9 Right-click over the text and click **Filter Effects**.

10 In the **Filter Effects** dialog:

- In the left **Effects** section, click to select the **Bevel and Emboss** check box.

- In the **Style** drop-down list, select **Emboss**.

- Set the **Blur** to 15.

- Set the **Depth** to 200.

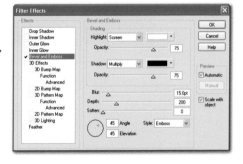

Create a Glass Effect

That's it! You can modify the transparency, colours, and emboss effects to further customize the effect, and group the objects to make a single object to work with.

Try placing an object behind your "glass" text to demonstrate its transparency.

Create a Warped Film Strip

Create a warped film strip using the **Envelope** tool.

In this exercise, you'll learn how to:

- Create a filmstrip out of basic Quick Shapes.

- Use the **Replicate** command to replicate an object.

- Use the **Envelope** and **Node** tools to distort a shape.

Create a Warped Film Strip

1 In the DrawPlus Startup Wizard, choose **Drawing**, select a page size of your choice and click **Open**.

2 On the left Drawing toolbar, on the Quick Shapes flyout, select the ▢ **Quick Rectangle**.

3 Draw a rectangle on the page, exactly 120 mm/4.7 in wide by 35 mm/1.4 in high. (You can set exact values on the **Transform** tab.)

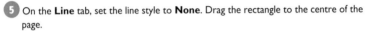

4 On the **Colour** or **Swatches** tab, set the fill colour to black.

5 On the **Line** tab, set the line style to **None**. Drag the rectangle to the centre of the page.

6 Draw another rectangle, this time a small one (4 mm/0.16 in x 3 mm/0.12 in).

7 Set the fill colour of the shape to white and set its line style to **None**. Drag the shape to just inside the upper left corner of the black rectangle.

Slide the node up to create a round-cornered lozenge shape. This is our first filmstrip 'hole.'

Now we'll create additional holes along the filmstrip edges.

8 Click the ⬉ **Pointer** tool and select the white lozenge shape. On the **Tools** menu, click **Replicate**.

9 In the **Replicate** dialog, in the **Grid Size** section:

- In the **Columns** box, type 18

- In the **Rows** box, type 1.

> 💡 If your replicated boxes extend over the end of the large rectangle, select the row of shapes and then use the size handles to resize the group.

10 In the **Replicate** dialog, in the **Spacing** section:

- Set the **X Spacing** value to 2.5 mm/0.1 in

- Set the **Y Spacing** value to 0.

- Click **OK**.

You'll now have a series of round-edged boxes along the top of the black rectangle.

11 Drag a rectangular selection box around the row of shapes, then click the ⊞ **Group** button to the lower right of the selection (or right-click the selection and then click **Group**).

Create a Warped Film Strip

12 With the group selected, hold down the **Ctrl** key and then drag to copy a second row of shapes to the lower edge of the black rectangle.

Now we'll repeat these steps to create the frames inside the strip of film.

13 Create a **Quick Rectangle** 18 mm/0.7 in wide x 23 mm/0.9 in high. Replicate it six times with an **X Spacing** value of 1.5 mm/0.06 in.

14 Position the new row of boxes inside the black rectangle. You will now have something resembling a filmstrip.

15 To complete the effect, add some Quick Shapes (or your own images) into the empty frames.

Now we'll apply the envelope.

16 Press **Ctrl+A** to select all the objects of the filmstrip, then click **Group**. On the **Tools** menu, click **Envelope Wizard**.

17 In the **Envelope Wizard** dialog, choose **Current Selection**, then click **Next**.

18 In the next dialog, scroll along to the right end of the gallery and select the final wave shape. Click **Finish**.

Now that we have a wavy filmstrip, we can distort the envelope by hand.

19 Click the ☐ **Node** tool and click on the filmstrip group to select it, revealing one node at each corner of the object.

Drag a selection box around the two left nodes to select them.

Create a Warped Film Strip

20 Drag down on either of the two selected nodes to move them both (you can press the **Shift** key to constrain the motion to the vertical plane).

As you drag, an outline is displayed to guide you.

Release the mouse button when you've achieved the desired shape.

In our final illustration, we've fine-tuned the distortion by dragging individual nodes, and adding a drop shadow with the **Shadow** tool.

Congratulations, you've finished your filmstrip!

In this exercise, we showed you how to create a simple image. The techniques used, however, can be implemented in any DrawPlus document. We're sure you'll find many other uses for the **Replicate** command and **Envelope** tool.

Here's another quick way to apply an envelope:

- On the Drawing toolbar, click the ⊠ **Envelope** tool, then on the Envelope context toolbar, select one of the presets from the drop-down flyout, or create your own custom envelope.

For more information, see the DrawPlus online Help.

Create Text on a Curve

In this tutorial, you'll create a company logo and make use of the DrawPlus Curve Text Wizard.

In this exercise, we'll show you how to:

- Use text and QuickShapes to create a basic logo.

- Apply a curved text preset to artistic text.

- Fine-tune a curved text object using the **Node** tool.

- Apply inner bevel, feather, and 3D effects.

Create Text on a Curve

1 In the DrawPlus Startup Wizard, choose **Drawing**, select a page size of your choice and click **Open**.

2 On the Drawing toolbar, on the Quick Shapes flyout, select the ⬭ **Quick Ellipse**. Drag out a circle about 90 mm/3.5 in across (hold down the **Ctrl** key to constrain the shape).

3 Use the **Line** and **Colour** tabs to apply a line style of **None** and a blue fill.

4 On the QuickShapes flyout, select a ⟳ **Quick Donut** and drag out a constrained 'annulus' 112 mm/4.4" across.

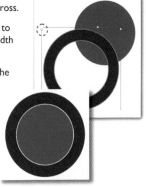

- Fill this shape with dark blue, set the line colour to white, and use the **Line** tab to adjust the line width to 2.5 pt.

- Drag the left node up to close the shape. Drag the top node to set a radius of 40 mm.

Now we'll centre the two objects.

5 Draw a selection bounding box to select both objects (or press **Ctrl + A**).

On the **Align** tab, select the **Include Page** check box and then click ⬚ **Horizontal Centre** and ⬚ **Vertical Centre** to centre the objects on the page.

6 Click the Λ **Artistic Text** tool, then click on the page and type to create an artistic text object.

Triple click the text to select it all. On the **Text** context toolbar set the text to **36pt Arial bold**.

Click the ⬉ **Pointer** tool and drag the object above your circles as illustrated.

7 Create a second artistic text object and format it as **24pt Arial bold**. Position this object beneath the circles.

Now to put each piece of text onto a curve...

8 Select the top text object.

On the **Text** context toolbar, on the ⬚ **Curved Text** flyout, click the ⌒ **Top Circle** preset.

9 At first, your text be too tightly curved to fit the circle, but it's easily adjusted.

10 Drag the text object down slightly so that its upper edge sits inside the darker blue ring. Apply a solid white fill from the **Swatches** tab.

11 Zoom into the text object and click the ▷ **Node** tool to reveal two square nodes, one at each end of the curved line of text.

Click and drag the nodes out to align the ends of the text inside the dark blue ring.

12 Use a combination of the following techniques to align the rest of the text inside the ring:

- Click and drag the curve segment to move it.

- Click and drag the control handles to change the slope of the curve.

13 Click the ▸ **Pointer** tool and select the lower text object.

On the Text context toolbar, on the **Curved Text** flyout, select the ⌣ **Bottom Circle** preset.

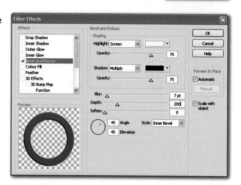

14 Move the text into the lower section of the ring; apply a white fill.

15 Repeat steps 11 and 12 to fit the text to the curve.

That's all there is to it!

To complete our logo, we used the ◈ **Fill** tool and applied some 𝑓𝑥 **Filter Effects**, as briefly explained below.

For more details, see online Help.

On the Quick Donut we applied:

- An **Inner Bevel** effect using a **Blur** of 7 pt and a **Depth of** 200.

Create Text on a Curve

On the inner circle we applied:

- A light-to-dark blue **Elliptical** fill.

- A **3D Effects** effect with a **Blur** of 100 pt and a **Depth** of 100 pt.

- A **Feather** effect using a **Blur** of 5 pt.

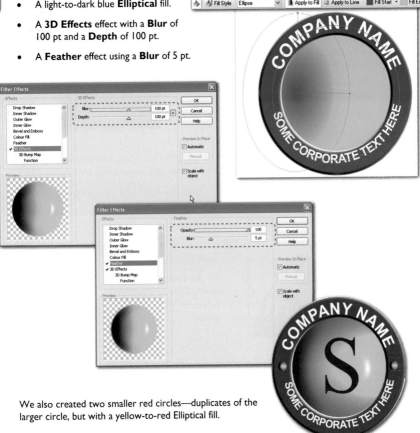

We also created two smaller red circles—duplicates of the larger circle, but with a yellow-to-red Elliptical fill.

You can also create your own path to apply text to.

1. Draw a line with the ✏ **Pencil** or 🖊 **Pen** tool, or create a QuickShape.

2. Select the drawn object and the text object together and choose **Tools/Curve Text Wizard**.

3. Click **Next** to start the Wizard. In the next screen, select the **Use current selection** check box to align the text with the drawn object.

Create a Wax Seal

In this tutorial, we'll show you how to create a 'wax seal' effect. You'll use some basic Quick Shapes and the **Freeform Paint** tool, then apply filter effects to add depth and dimension to your shapes.

Once you've created your basic wax seal, you can get creative and adapt it for a multitude of purposes.

You'll learn how to:

- Create Quick Shapes.

- Use the **Freeform Paint** tool.

- Use the **Colour** and **Line** tabs to apply properties to a shape.

- Use the **Filter Effects** dialog to apply bevel and emboss effects.

- Work with grouped objects.

Create a Wax Seal

1 In the DrawPlus Startup Wizard, choose **Drawing**, select a page size of your choice and click **Open**.

2 On the Drawing toolbar, on the Quick Shapes flyout, click the ○ **Quick Ellipse**, then hold down the **Ctrl** key and draw a circle about 10 cm in diameter.

Let's now add a red fill to our circle.

3 On the **Colour** tab, click the **Fill** button, and apply a red fill to your shape by clicking a point in the red section of the colour wheel.

4 On the **Line** tab, remove the outline from your shape by selecting **None** from the line style drop-down list.

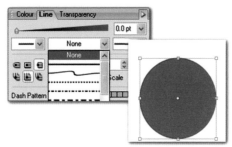

> Once you've selected your colour hue from the colour wheel, you can adjust its **saturation** and **lightness** by clicking and dragging the small circle inside the inner HSL Wheel.

5 On the Drawing toolbar, click the ✐ **Freeform Paint** tool.

6 On the context toolbar, select the round nib shape and increase the width to 30 pt.

7 Click and drag at various points around your circle to create an uneven border.

8 Increase the brush width to 60 pt and then click to add a few larger circular shapes to the border.

You can vary the brush width, and the click and drag/click process as much as you want to achieve the desired effect.

Now it's time to get creative.

9 When you're happy with your finished shape, on the **Edit** menu, click **Select All**, then on the Standard toolbar, click  **Add** to combine all of the shapes into one.

Don't worry if your shape doesn't look exactly like our illustration—no two wax 'blobs' are alike!

At the moment, the shape doesn't look very impressive, but once we've added a bevel and emboss effect, it will start to resemble the wax seal we're hoping to achieve.

10 Select your shape and then on the Drawing toolbar, click *fx* **Filter Effects**. In the **Filter Effects** dialog, in the **Effects** list, select **Bevel and Emboss**.

In the **Bevel and Emboss** section, set the following values:

- **Blur:** 21

- **Depth:** 123

- **Angle:** 45

- **Elevation:** 45

- **Style:** Inner Bevel

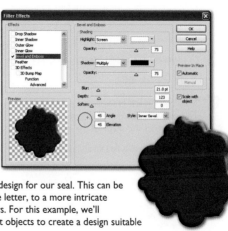

The preview pane updates to show you the effect these settings have on your shape.

When you're happy with your settings, click **OK**.

We're now ready to create the design for our seal. This can be anything you want, from a simple letter, to a more intricate combination of shapes and letters. For this example, we'll combine a Quick Shape with text objects to create a design suitable for use on wedding stationery.

11 On the Quick Shapes flyout, click the ◯ **Quick Ellipse**, hold down the **Ctrl** key and draw a circle inside your wax blob. Apply the same red fill you used before and remove the outline.

12 Right-click the new circle and choose **Filter Effects**.

In the **Filter Effects** dialog, select **Bevel and Emboss** and set the following values:

- **Blur:** 3.5

- **Depth:** 195

- **Angle:** 45

- **Elevation:** 45

- **Style:** Inner Bevel

Create a Wax Seal

13 Repeat step 11 to create a second slightly smaller circle. Centre it inside the first one. Again, apply the same red fill and remove the outline.

14 Repeat step 12 and in the **Filter Effects** dialog, select **Bevel and Emboss** and set the following values:

- **Blur:** 3.5

- **Depth:** 195

- **Angle:** 230

- **Elevation:** 45

- **Style:** Outer Bevel

15 To complete the design, simply add Quick Shapes and initials to the centre of the seal.

Here's how we did it:

16 Draw two **Quick Hearts** and position them one inside the other. (We dragged the sliding node to adjust the shape of the heart slightly.)

- Apply the same red fill and remove the outlines.

- For the outermost heart, apply an **inner bevel**. Use the same settings applied in step 12, but increase the **Blur** value to 5.

- For the inner heart, apply an **outer bevel**. Use the same settings applied in step 14, but increase the **Blur** value to 5.

17 Use the Λ **Artistic Text** tool to create two text objects, each containing a single letter. Select

- Select a text object, and on the Text context toolbar, apply an appropriate font style and size. We used **36 pt Arial**.

- On the **Swatches** tab, apply the same red you've been using throughout this tutorial.

- In the **Filter Effects** dialog, add an **inner bevel** with the following settings:

  Blur: 2; **Depth:** 150; **Angle:** 230; **Elevation:** 45.

- Drag each letter into the heart, using the ↻ **Rotate** tool to rotate them into position.

Create a Wax Seal

18 For the finishing touch, use the **Quick Petal** to add some small flowers to the lower section of the heart. We applied an **inner bevel** with the following settings:

> It's surprising just how useful those Quick Shapes can be! Don't forget to explore the various options on the Quick Shape flyout.

Blur: 1; **Depth:** 100; **Angle:** 45; **Elevation:** 45.

19 Finally, it's a good idea to group all the elements of your seal—click **Edit/Select All** (or press **Ctrl+A**), then click the 🔳 **Group** button to the lower right of the selection (or right-click and select **Group**).

Congratulations, you've created your first wax seal!

As you can see, the entire process mainly consists of creating and manipulating Quick Shapes and text objects, and then applying bevel and emboss effects to them.

Once you've mastered these techniques, you can create any design you want. Below are a couple of examples to get you started.

> All of these examples are in our sample file, **Wax Seal.dpp,** which you'll find in the **Workspace** folder of your DrawPlus installation directory—normally located at: **C:\Program Files\Serif\DrawPlus\X2\Tutorials\Workspace.**

Create a Gel Button

If you're an Internet user, you'll no doubt have seen these 'gel' style buttons. Although they look impressive, they are surprisingly simple to create in DrawPlus.

In this tutorial, you'll apply transparency, gradient fills, and filter effects to multi-layered shapes to create striking gel buttons. You'll learn how to:

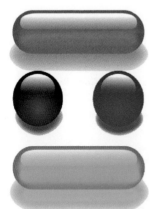

- Create and manipulate Quick Shapes.

- Use the **Colour** and **Line** tabs to apply properties to a shape.

- Work with gradient transparency.

- Use the **Filter Effects** dialog to apply feather effects.

- Group and ungroup objects.

Our gel button samples are provided in the **Gel Buttons.dpp** file, which you'll find in the **Workspace** folder of your DrawPlus installation directory—normally located at:

C:\Program Files\Serif\DrawPlus\X2\Tutorials\Workspace

Create a Gel Button

Our illustration shows what we are aiming to achieve in this tutorial—a translucent gel button with a shadow. We'll show you how simple it is to create this in DrawPlus.

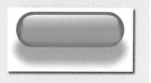

1. In the DrawPlus Startup Wizard, choose **Drawing**, select a page size of your choice and click **Open**.

2. On the left Drawing toolbar, on the Quick Shapes flyout, click the ☐ **Quick Rectangle**, then click and drag to draw a large rectangle on your page.

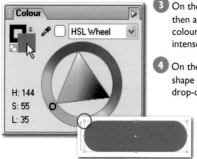

3. On the **Colour** tab, click the **Fill** button, and then apply a fill colour by clicking a point in the colour wheel. For optimum effect, choose a fairly intense colour—we used a mid green.

4. On the **Line** tab, remove the outline from your shape by selecting **None** from the line style drop-down list.

5. Drag the left sliding node all the way up to the top to round the corners fully.

6. Click the ▶ **Pointer** tool, then right-click the shape and choose **Copy**. Right-click again and choose **Paste**.

The new shape is pasted on top of the original and is selected by default.

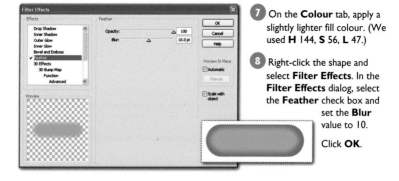

7. On the **Colour** tab, apply a slightly lighter fill colour. (We used **H** 144, **S** 56, **L** 47.)

8. Right-click the shape and select **Filter Effects**. In the **Filter Effects** dialog, select the **Feather** check box and set the **Blur** value to 10.

Click **OK**.

Create a Gel Button

9 Copy and paste this new shape and apply an even lighter colour fill (we used **H** 144, **S** 79, **L** 51). Open the **Filter Effects** dialog again and increase the **Blur** value to 14.

10 With the new rectangle selected, click its upper size handle and drag down to make a thinner shape.

We now have our 'glowing' gel button, but we still need to add a reflection highlight.

11 Copy and paste the original shape and apply a white fill. This new shape will completely cover the three previous layers.

> 💡 If you want to create a gel button that you can quickly recolour, use **linked colours**. For more information, see the online Help, or the "Create a Velvet Effect" Level 1 tutorial.

In order to create our reflection effect, we need to edit this white shape using the 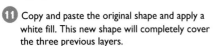 **Node** tool. To do this, we must first convert the object to curves.

12 With the white shape selected, on the Standard toolbar, click 🔘 **Convert to Curves**.

13 Click the 🔺 **Node** tool and draw a selection bounding box around the two nodes at the lower edge of the shape.

Click on one of the nodes and drag it up slightly—the other node will also move.

14 Repeat the previous step to move the upper two nodes.

15 Now click the 🔸 **Pointer** tool, select the white shape, and reduce its size slightly.

Position the shape in the upper centre area of the button.

Our button looks very effective already. However, with another couple of steps we can make it look even more realistic.

We want to soften the highlight slightly, at the lower edge only. We'll use a gradient transparency to achieve this effect.

16 With the reflection selected, on the Drawing toolbar, click the 💡 **Transparency** tool and draw a transparency path from just above to just below the shape.

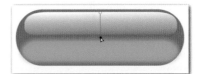

Create a Gel Button

> Transparency effects are great for highlights, shading and shadows, and simulating 'rendered' realism. They can make the critical difference between flat-looking illustrations and images with depth and snap.
>
> Transparency may seem a bit tricky because by definition, you can't see it the way you can see a colour fill applied to an object. In fact, it's there all the time in DrawPlus. Each new object has a transparency property: the default just happens to be 'None'—that is, no transparency (opaque).

Congratulations, you've created your gel button. Now to add a shadow. This is an important step because it gives the button a translucent appearance.

17 Click the ⬆ **Pointer** tool and select the original large shape from your button—you may need to hold down the **Alt** key and click a few times to get to this particular shape. Copy and paste the shape and move it away from the button.

18 Right-click the shape and select **Filter Effects**. Select the **Feather** check box and set the **Blur** value to 13.

19 Copy and paste this new shape, make it smaller and lighter in colour, and position it on top of the shadow base.

20 Now select both of your shadow objects and move them into place beneath your gel button.

That's all there is to it! We hope you'll agree that the process of creating this gel button is actually a fairly simple one, but the results are very effective.

> It's a good idea to 'group' the various objects in your drawing. When objects are grouped, you can position, resize, rotate, or shear them at the same time. The objects that comprise a group are intact, but can also be edited individually.
>
> In our gel button example, we grouped all the shapes that make up the button, and then grouped the two 'shadow' shapes. Once we had moved the shadow into place, we grouped everything together.
>
> **To create a group:**
>
> - Select the objects you want to group, then to the lower right of the selection, click the ⊞ **Group** button (or right-click and choose **Group**).
>
> **To ungroup (turn a group back into a multiple selection)**
>
> - Click the ⊞ **Ungroup** button (or right-click and choose **Ungroup**).
>
> **To edit an object contained within a group:**
>
> - Press and hold down the **Ctrl** key and then click to select the object.

Create a Torn Paper Effect

In this tutorial, you will combine DrawPlus tools and techniques to make a variety of torn paper effects—including a pirate's treasure map.

You'll learn how to:

- Draw lines and shapes with the **Pencil** tool.

- Combine shapes using the **Subtract** command.

- Use the **Roughen** tool to turn smooth edges into jagged outlines.

- Apply bitmap fills and paper textures.

- Use the **Filter Effects** dialog to create a drop shadow.

Create a Torn Paper Effect

1 In the DrawPlus Startup Wizard, click **Drawing**, select a page size of your choice, click **Open**.

2 On the left Drawing toolbar, on the Quick Shapes flyout, click the ☐ **Quick Rectangle**, then draw a large rectangle on your page. This rectangle will be your 'piece of paper.'

3 On the Drawing toolbar, click the ✏ **Pencil** tool and draw a jagged line to represent the torn edge of the paper **(Figure 1)**.

Connect the start and end nodes by continuing the line outside the edge of the rectangle **(Figure 2)**.

When you release the mouse button, your new shape will sit on top of the rectangle, hiding its edge **(Figure 3)**.

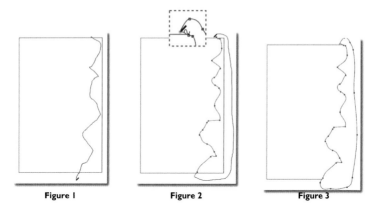

| Figure 1 | Figure 2 | Figure 3 |

Q Curve Smoothness controls

These display in the **Context toolbar** when you select the **Pencil** tool (click the arrow to the right of the value box to display the slider). Use these controls to refine the curve most recently drawn with the **Pencil** tool (as long as the line is still selected).

- Increase the value in the box, or drag the slider to the right, to simplify the line by decreasing the number of nodes. The fewer the nodes, the more the resulting line will deviate from the original line drawn.

- Decrease the value in the box, or drag the slider to the left, to make the curve more complex by increasing the number of nodes. The greater the number of nodes, the more closely the resulting line will be to the original line drawn

The more nodes there are on a line or shape, the more control you have over the shape. The fewer nodes there are, the simpler (smoother) the line or shape.

Create a Torn Paper Effect

4 If necessary, on the Context toolbar, adjust the smoothness of your line with the **Smoothness** controls.

5 On the **Edit** menu, choose **Select All** (or press **Ctrl + A**) to select both the rectangle and the freehand shape.

6 On the Standard toolbar, click the  **Subtract** button. DrawPlus removes the section of the rectangle that is overlapped by the freehand shape.

Now that we've got the basic outline for our piece of torn paper, there are a multitude of things we can do with it. We'll show you a few examples then we'll let you experiment on your own...

Example 1: Newspaper

To achieve this effect we applied one of DrawPlus's predefined bitmap fills to the shape, and then added a drop-shadow.

To apply a bitmap fill

1 Select the shape, and then on the **Swatches** tab, click the **Bitmap** category drop-down list and choose **Misc**.

2 Click the **misc06** swatch to apply it to your shape.

3 On the **Line** tab, in the line style drop-down list, remove the shape's outline by selecting **None**.

To create a drop shadow

1 Right-click the shape and select **Filter Effects**.

2 In the **Filter Effects** dialog, select the **Drop Shadow** check box and then set the following values:

- **Opacity:** 35
- **Blur:** 4.5
- **Distance:** 3.5
- **Angle:** 135

Click **OK**.

Create a Torn Paper Effect

Example 2: Marbled
Simple but effective, this marbled effect was created by applying and editing a plasma fill.

We also removed the outline and applied a drop shadow.

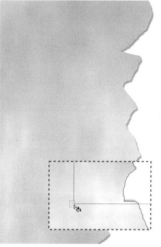

To apply and edit a plasma fill

1 Select the shape and then click the **Swatches** tab.

2 On the **Swatches** tab, in the ▨ ▾ **Gradient** category drop-down list, choose **Plasma**.

3 Apply any gradient fill by clicking its swatch.

4 With the shape still selected, on the Drawing toolbar, click the ✦ **Fill** tool. The shape's fill path and nodes display.

5 On the **Swatches** tab, replace the colours of the fill by dragging from a colour swatch to the nodes.

Example 3: Rough edge
The simplest method of all—we quickly roughened the edge of this piece of paper using the **Roughen** tool. Again, we completed the effect with a drop shadow.

1 Select the shape, remove its outline, and apply the fill of your choice.

2 On the Drawing toolbar, click the ▨ **Roughen** tool, then click on your shape and drag in any direction. The further you drag, the more pronounced the effect.

To remove a roughen effect from an object, double-click it with the **Roughen** tool, or click **Remove Roughen Effect** on the context toolbar.

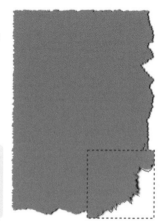

📖 Only the outline of the shape is affected and there's no internal distortion—so if you have applied a bitmap fill, for example, the fill remains intact.

Create a Torn Paper Effect

Example 4: Treasure map

Our final example is a pirate's treasure map, which we created using a variety of DrawPlus tools and features. We'll explain how we did it; however, rather than replicating our example, you should have fun with this and explore your own ideas.

You'll find our map, **Treasure Map.dpp**, in the **Tutorials\Workspace** folder of your DrawPlus installation, normally located in **C:\Program Files\Serif\DrawPlus\X2\Tutorials\Workspace**. The individual elements are on **Layer 2** of the treasure map—you'll need to make **Layer 2** visible and the active layer.

Burnt edge effect

We wanted the edges of our map to look charred.

To accomplish this, in the **Filter Effects** dialog, we added an **Inner Glow** using the following settings:

Blend Mode: Normal

Opacity: 75

Blur: 50 pt

Intensity: 15

Colour: Dark brown —RGB(42, 32, 15)

Tents

We used the **Straight Line** tool to draw the campsite.

River and paths

These were drawn with the **Pen** tool.

The river is a simple curved line, with a weight of 7.5 pt.

We applied drop shadow and feather filter effects to soften the edges.

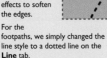

For the footpaths, we simply changed the line style to a dotted line on the **Line** tab.

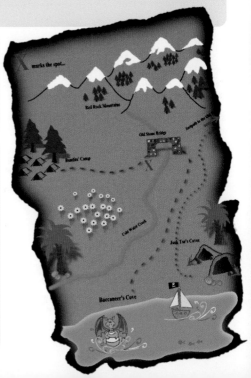

Create a Torn Paper Effect

Mountains

We used the **Pencil** tool to draw the mountain range. The snowy peaks were created as separate objects. We applied a drop shadow filter effect to each element to create a 3D effect.

Trees

We drew our fir and palm trees with the **Pencil** tool.

We drew the first tree, applied colour and a drop shadow, then we used copy and paste to replicate the original, resizing where necessary.

Flowers

We made these with simple **Quick Petals**.

The stalks were drawn with the **Straight Line** tool, and the leaves are **Quick Ellipses**.

Fish

We used the **Pencil** tool for the body, and a **Quick Ellipse** for the eye.

Caves

For the cave entrances, we used the **Pencil** tool, connecting the start and end nodes to make a closed shape. We then applied a gradient fill to the shapes.

Pirate Ship

A combination of shapes, lines, and fills was used to create our pirate ship.

Dragon

Our friendly dragon was created with the **Pencil** tool.

Create a Torn Paper Effect

Other suggestions...
DrawPlus provides you with a number of other fills and textures that are particularly suitable for creating paper effects.

On the Layers tab:

- Click 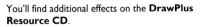 **Apply Paper Texture**, then choose from the wide selection of textures available in the **Bitmap Selector** dialog.

On the Swatches tab:

- Click the **Gradient** category drop-down list and experiment with the **Plasma**, **Four Colour**, and **Three Colour** categories. You can create very different results just by editing the colours and the gradient of the fill path, and adjusting transparency.

- Click the **Bitmap** category drop-down list and explore the **Bitmap/Material** category.

  Try applying various fills, then on the **Transparency** tab, reduce the opacity to 50% to create an interesting paper texture.

You'll find additional effects on the **DrawPlus Resource CD**.

For example, on the **Effects** tab:

- For a 3D effect, apply the **Card** effect in the **Cloth and Paper** category.

- Scroll through the swatches in the **Designer** category. We particularly like **Texture**, **Fine Contours**, and **Paper Bag**.

  Finally, why not try combining fills *and* effects for some really unique paper textures—don't forget to adjust the transparency setting too!

As you can see, once you have created the basic template for your torn paper, there are many things you can do with it. This tutorial has illustrated a few ideas, but we hope it has also inspired you to explore some of your own.

Create a Wine Glass

Create a wine glass you can place on any background to show its transparency. We've created sample objects for you, but if you want to try this on your own you'll need to be (or become) familiar with the various line drawing tools.

You'll learn how to:

- Apply simple fills and transparencies using the **Swatches** and **Transparency** tabs.

- Use the **Transparency** tool to adjust the transparency of an object.

- Turn a basic line drawing into a realistic 3D image.

Create a Wine Glass

1 In the DrawPlus Startup Wizard, under **Open**, choose **Saved Work**, browse to the **Tutorials\Workspace** folder and open the **Wine Glass.dpp** file. In a standard installation, you'll find this folder in the following location:

C:\Program Files\Serif\DrawPlus\X2\Tutorials\Workspace

The first page of the document shows a **keyline** (line drawing) of the wine glass, and the last page the finished article. In between pages are labelled in stages.

To navigate between pages, click the ◀ **Previous Page** and ▶ **Next Page** buttons on the HintLine toolbar.

2 Save the file under a new name, so you can work on it without altering the original.

On the HintLine toolbar, click the 🗒 **Page Manager** and delete pages 2 to 7.

Reopen the original file and keep it available for reference while you're working on the other (use the **Window/Tile** command or adjust the windows for convenience).

For this tutorial we'll remove any elements that aren't required, and bring it all together at the end. We'll begin with the top of the glass and work our way down. Since the wine glass is in keyline form to start with, you will only be able to select an element by clicking on the line itself.

3 **(See Wine Glass.dpp, Stage 1)**
Click the keyline of the 'bowl' to select the shape that corresponds to **1** in **illustration A**. This shape has a light background colour.

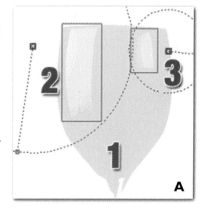

- On the **Swatches** and **Transparency** tabs, apply a black fill and a solid 10% opacity.

- Remove the keyline (outline)—on the **Line** tab, in the line style drop-down list, select **None**.

4 Select the left 'strip glow' (labelled **2** in **illustration A**) and colour it solid white.

5 On the **Transparency** tab, in the 🔲▾ **Gradient** drop-down list, select **Radial** and apply a radial transparency (we used **Radial 21**). Use the 🔲 **Transparency** tool to adjust the transparency so its path looks like our illustration. Remove any keyline.

6 Repeat the previous step for the smaller strip glow (**A/3**).

7 **(See Stage 2)** Copy the strip glow 2 and paste it over itself—this trick gives a sharper transparency. Do the same with element 3, but after pasting it, nudge it slightly to the left. This will give the glass depth, as if light is reflecting from the inside as well.

8 Select the main bowl **(1)**, copy and paste it, then give it a white fill—it will be nearly invisible but that's the effect we want. Make it slightly smaller by dragging fractionally inward from the top left and then from the bottom right.

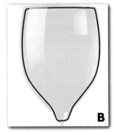

The bowl shape should now sit in front of the other bowl, hiding most of it. In **illustration B**, we've given the shape a false outline to illustrate its position.

B

> We made the new 'clear' bowl slightly smaller than the original so that a bit of grey is revealed at the edges, lending a believable outline.

In the next series of steps, we'll give this new bowl object some local transparency and then replicate it a number of times so it can contribute transparency in different places.

9 With the new bowl object selected, apply the **Ellipse 19** transparency.

10 Click the 🏆 **Transparency** tool and using **illustration C/1** as a guide, position the transparency outside the object's right edge, slightly overlapping it to create a feathered soft edge. (In the illustration, the reddish zone indicates the overlap.)

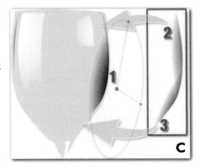

C

In the overlap zone, you should see a blending into white where less transparency reveals the new bowl's white colour. We'll duplicate this object and adjust the transparency on each copy to extend the feathered edge.

11 Copy and paste the current bowl in place, then drag its transparency zone up so it affects the area labelled **C/2**.

12 Repeat the paste operation and this time adjust transparency downwards to **C/3**.

Now you'll see a consistent white blend that follows the side of the glass. We'll use the same 'bowl' to add transparency in a couple of other areas.

Create a Wine Glass

13 Paste again, but this time remove the fill colour (on the **Colour** tab, click the top left swatch) and apply a solid white line (right-click the white swatch and select **Apply to Line**). On the **Line** tab, ensure that the line thickness is 1pt.

14 Drag the transparency (not the object!) up to the top left area, as shown in **illustration D**, and reshape it slightly to produce a light-reflective keyline that adds definition.

15 Copy and paste the object created in the previous step (to preserve its fill and line) and move the copy over to the right. Enlarge it as in **E** to create a stronger line down the side of the glass.

The next few operations are more of the same, in that we're adding a few more reflective transparencies—but these will be small 'flares' around the rim, front, side, and base of the glass. In **illustration E** we've coloured them black for emphasis, but yours will be white.

16 **(Stage 3)** For **E/1**, **E/2**, and **E/3**, create small white-filled circles with no line, flatten and stretch them as needed. Apply any elliptical transparency with resizing and adjustment to achieve the desired flare effects in very specific places.

17 For **E/4**, we used a simple radial transparency on a freehand shape.

18 At **E/5**, to finish off the top half, we added a small curved line that defines the base of the bowl. Applying transparencies to single lines is just the same as for shapes—in this case we used another elliptical transparency.

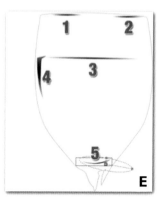

Against a coloured background, you should now have something closely resembling illustration **F**.

Now we'll follow similar procedures for the base and stem. The basic approach is to apply a light base colour and then side highlights, followed by the flares to add realism. We'll concentrate more on speed than detail, to avoid repetition. Don't forget to remove keylines unless otherwise stated.

19 **(See Stage 4)** Select the keyline that defines the stem (**illustration G/1**), which will be using the original light background colour. Apply a black fill and solid 10% opacity. Copy and paste it in place, fill the copy with white, and add a 1pt white line.

20 Using **G/2** as a guide, apply an elliptical transparency to the object and move the transparency (not the object) to the right of the stem, with a slight overlap. This effect will resemble what we achieved in **illustration C**.

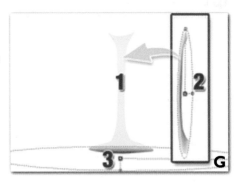

21 Copy the object and paste it again, so it retains its white fill and line, then rotate the transparency and extend it to resemble **G/3**. This will give the base of the stem a reflective glow.

To finish off we'll apply the flares to the stem in the same manner we used in step 16 (**illustration E**).

22 **(Stage 5)** You should still have a copy of the stem on the Clipboard, so paste it again and nudge it slightly to the right. Remove its fill colour but keep the white line. Apply a large radial transparency, similar in size to **G/2**, but circular as shown in **illustration H/1**. This should create a fine sliver down the left side of the stem, to give it more definition.

23 Copy and paste **E/5**, the line defining the base of the bowl, then drag the copy down to define the base of the stem where it starts to form the foot (**H/2**).

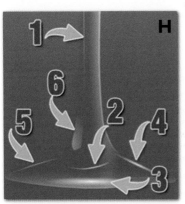

24 Repeat the copy/paste operation using the shape from **E/1**, moving this copy down to the very base and enlarging it to fill the full width as in **H/3**. Paste the same object again, and using **H/4** as reference place the copy to the right of the stem and rotate it to follow the contour. Repeat the paste-and-adjust step for **H/5**.

25 Finally, for **H/6** apply a radial transparency to the existing shape at that location, and move the transparency below and right so that the top of the shape is blended.

Create a Wine Glass

Congratulations! Now that you've mastered this technique, why not try applying the same methods to other objects like glass buttons for the Web; or use the skills you've learned to create shiny metallic objects and water effects.

Turn Quick Shapes into Fruit

This quick and easy tutorial will show you how to turn a simple shape into a piece of fruit!

In this exercise, you will:

- Create Quick Shapes.

- Use the **Pen** tool.

- Use the **Node** tool to transform shapes and lines.

- Apply and adjust gradient fills.

- Apply a drop shadow effect.

Turn Quick Shapes into Fruit

- In the Startup Wizard, choose **Drawing**, select a page size of your choice and click **Open**. We'll draw a few different fruit shapes, let's begin with a pear.

To draw a pear

1 On the Drawing toolbar, on the Quick Shapes flyout, click the ○ **Quick Ellipse** and draw an ellipse on your page.

> To constrain the shape, press and hold the **Ctrl** key while you draw. (You don't need perfect shapes for this exercise however.)

2 On the Drawing toolbar, click the ▷ **Node** tool.

3 With the shape selected, on the Standard toolbar, click ◎ **Convert to Curves**. You'll see four 'nodes' appear on the circle's edge.

Converting a shape to curves allows you to edit it using the **Node** tool and the **Curves context toolbar**.

- To change the shape of an object that has been converted to curves, click one of its nodes and then drag it to a new position.

- To add a node, click a line segment with the **Node** tool to add a new node at that point.

- To delete a node, select it with the **Node** tool and press the **Delete** key or click the ⚏ **Delete Node** button on the Context toolbar.

4 Use the **Node** tool to add and move nodes, until your shape resembles a pear.

If you're having trouble with this step, you can use our sample file, **Pear.dpp**, which you'll find in the **Workspace** folder of your DrawPlus installation directory—normally located at:

C:\Program Files\Serif\DrawPlus\X2\ Tutorials\Workspace.

5 Click the ▶ **Pointer** tool. Your shape is automatically selected.

6 On the Swatches tab, in the ▨ ▾ **Gradient** drop-down list, select the **Linear** category and apply any yellow/green fill by clicking its swatch. We used **Linear 185**.

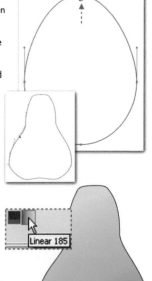

Turn Quick Shapes into Fruit

If you want to change the colour or gradient of the fill path, you can do so by using the **Fill** tool. We'll show you how to do this next, but if you're happy with the colour of your pear you can skip the following step.

7 On the Drawing toolbar, click the **Fill** tool.

Depending on the type of fill you selected (linear, radial, ellipse, etc.), you'll see the fill path displayed as one or more lines, with nodes marking where the spectrum between each key colour begins and ends.

You can edit the fill path by:

- Dragging the nodes to change the spread of colours between nodes.
- Changing, adding, or deleting key colours.

To change the colour spread

Drag the start and end path nodes, or click on the object for a new start node and drag out a new fill path. The gradient starts where you place the start node, and ends where you place the end node.

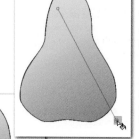

To change a key colour

Click its node, then click a colour swatch.

- or -

Drag from a colour swatch on to any node to change the key colour of the node. Note that the node doesn't need to be selected.

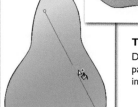

To add a key colour

Drag from a colour swatch on to a portion of the fill path where there is no node. The cursor changes to include a plus (+) sign.

When dragging from colour swatches to nodes, make sure the tip of the pointer is over the node or path (watch the cursor) when you release the mouse button. Otherwise the colour will be applied to the whole object as a solid fill.

To delete a key colour

Select a colour node and press **Delete**.

Turn Quick Shapes into Fruit

8 On the **Line** tab, remove the outline from the pear by selecting **None** from the line style drop-down list.

To complete the pear, all we need to do now is draw the stalk.

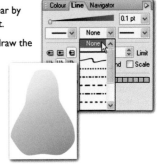

9 On the Drawing toolbar, click the 🖊 **Pen** tool and then draw the outline of the stalk on your page.

Be sure to connect the first and last nodes to create an enclosed shape.

10 Click the ➤ **Pointer** tool, then on the **Colour** or **Swatches** tab, apply a dark green line and fill to the shape.

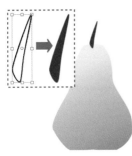

11 Finally, drag the stalk into position on top of the pear.

For a touch of realism, we'll use the **Shadow** tool to add a drop shadow effect.

To add a drop shadow

1 On the **Edit** menu, choose **Select All** (or press **Ctrl + A**), then to the lower right of the selection, click 🔳 **Group**.

2 With the pear selected, on the Drawing toolbar, click the 🔲 **Shadow** tool.

On the Shadow context toolbar, set the following values, pressing the **Enter** key after each one:

- **Opacity:** 25
- **Blur:** 17
- **Shear X:** 7
- **Scale X:** 155%
- **Scale Y:** 50%

(You can also drag the various Shadow tool nodes to adjust the effect.)

Turn Quick Shapes into Fruit

You've created your first fruit shape. We think you'll agree that this was a very simple process. Let's now try our hand at drawing a watermelon slice.

To draw a watermelon slice

1. On the Quick Shapes flyout, click the ○ **Quick Ellipse** and draw an ellipse on your page.

2. With the shape selected, drag the left node down to almost the halfway point.

3. On the Standard toolbar, click ○ **Convert to Curves**.

4. Hover the cursor just outside one of the corners of the shape. When the cursor changes to the Rotate cursor, rotate the shape by clicking and dragging one of the rotate handles.

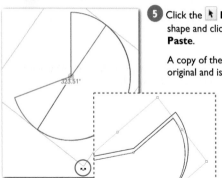

5. Click the ▶ **Pointer** tool, then right-click your shape and click **Copy**. Right-click again and click **Paste**.

   A copy of the shape is pasted on top of the original and is selected by default.

6. Make this new shape slightly smaller than the original by dragging one of its corner size handles towards the centre.

7. Place the shapes so that they match up along the cut edge of the slice.

8. Select the large shape, then on the **Swatches** tab, apply a dark green fill and outline.

9. Select the small shape, then on the **Swatches** tab, in the 🔲 ▾ **Gradient** drop-down list, select **Radial** and apply an orange/red fill—we used **Radial 154**.

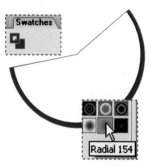

Turn Quick Shapes into Fruit

10 On the **Line** tab, remove the outline by selecting **None** from the line style drop-down list.

Now all that remains is to add some seeds...

11 Create a narrow ellipse and fill it with an appropriate radial fill.

We used **Radial 155** and added a white node to the fill path. We also adjusted the angle of the fill path slightly.

12 Copy and paste this shape to make additional seeds. Rotate the seeds and vary their positions inside the watermelon slice.

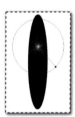

13 Add a drop shadow and you're done!

You can use this basic method to draw any other kind of fruit or vegetable.

The banana is slightly more complicated, however, so we'll break it down for you...

💡 If you want to dissect this image for yourself, you'll find the sample file, **Banana.dpp**, in the **Tutorials\Workspace** folder of your DrawPlus installation directory.

To draw a banana

This section explains how we drew our banana; however, don't feel you have to use the same method. Experiment with the various tools and techniques that DrawPlus has to offer—you may find a better way to create the same effect.

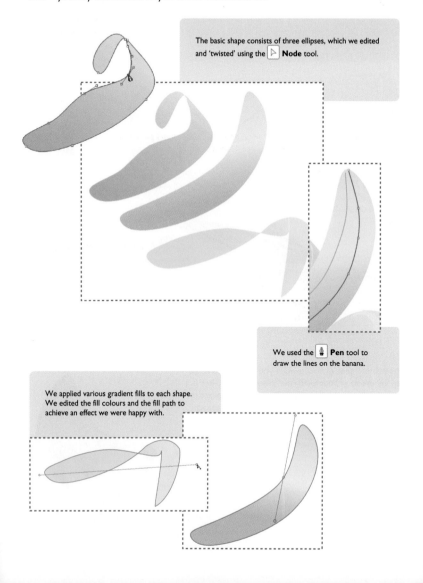

The basic shape consists of three ellipses, which we edited and 'twisted' using the ▷ **Node** tool.

We used the 🖊 **Pen** tool to draw the lines on the banana.

We applied various gradient fills to each shape. We edited the fill colours and the fill path to achieve an effect we were happy with.

Turn Quick Shapes into Fruit

The shading effects on the banana and skin were created with the 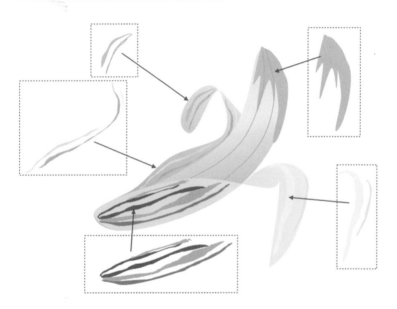 **Pencil** tool. We created closed shapes by connecting the start and end nodes, and then applied various solid and gradient fills.

As you can see, with DrawPlus you don't need to be an expert to produce effective results. All it takes is a few simple shapes, lines, and fills, and a little practice. Once you've drawn your individual fruit shapes, you can group them any way you like to create interesting still-life compositions.

Draw a Gemstone

In this tutorial, we'll make use of layers to keep different sections of our drawing intact. We'll also be combining various DrawPlus tools and techniques so if you're a new user, you might want to try some of the earlier tutorials before beginning this one.

In particular, it will help if you are somewhat familiar with layers and with line tools and node editing—we'll outline the basic principles here, but for more detailed information see online Help.

In this exercise, you will:

- Work with the **Layers** tab.

- Use Quick Shapes and lines to create custom shapes.

- Use the **Node** tool to edit lines and shapes.

- Apply gradient fills.

- Create custom fills and add them to the DrawPlus Gallery.

- Apply transparency.

Draw a Gemstone

You'll find our sample file—**Gem.dpp**—in the **Tutorials\Workspace** folder of your DrawPlus installation, which is normally located at:

C:\Program Files\Serif\DrawPlus\X2\Tutorials\Workspace.

The file consists of four layers:

Layers 1, 2, and 3 form the finished gemstone. You will create your own versions of these layers in this tutorial.

Layer 4 illustrates the various stages involved in the creation of the gemstone. This layer is hidden by default so you'll need to make it visible.

The gemstone design we're going to create is fairly complex, so this tutorial is an ideal opportunity to work with layers. Before we begin, let's go over some basic concepts...

By default, all new DrawPlus documents consist of a single layer. Objects created on this layer are stacked in order, from back to front, with each new object in front of the others. For simple designs, one layer is usually sufficient, but if you're working on a complex design it makes sense to separate groups of objects on different layers. This allows you to work on one layer at a time without disturbing elements on other layers.

The **Layers** tab displays all the layers in a document and their properties (you can turn these on or off by clicking the appropriate button). The hierarchical tree view displays thumbnail previews of the objects on each layer.

- To display the objects contained on a layer, click the + sign to the left of the layer to expand it.

- To see a larger preview of an object, hover over a thumbnail preview.

- To select an object on the page, click it's thumbnail.

- The coloured line under each layer's properties buttons indicates the colour of the

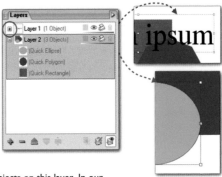

selection 'bounding box' of all objects on this layer. In our illustration, selected objects on **Layer 1** display with a blue selection bounding box; objects on **Layer 2** display with a red bounding box.

- Use the buttons at the bottom of the **Layers** tab to add and delete layers, change the layer order, edit all, and/or view all layers.

You'll learn more about layers as you work through this exercise, so let's get started.

To create a document and add layers

1 In the DrawPlus Startup Wizard, choose **Drawing**, select a page size of your choice and click **Open**.

2 On the **Layers** tab, right-click **Layer 1** and select **Layer Properties**.

In the **Layer Properties** dialog, in the **Name:** box, type 'Pavilion' and click **OK**.

(To change the colour of the selection bounding box for this layer, click the colour swatch to open the **Colour Picker**.)

3 On the **Layers** tab, click the ⬧ **Add Layer** button. Name this second layer 'Crown' and click **OK**.

4 Repeat the previous step to add a third layer named 'Table.'

Your layers should be in the same sequence as ours. If they're not, you can reorder them by clicking on a layer, and then clicking ⬆ **Move Layer Up** or ⬇ **Move Layer Down**.

5 On the **File** menu, click **Save** and save your document as **Gem.dpp**.

Now let's begin by creating the basic outline of the pavilion section.

Gem nomenclature

If you're wondering why we've named our layers 'Pavilion,' 'Crown,' and 'Table,' here's the reason...

When discussing faceted gems, the bottom is called the pavilion; the top section is called the crown; and the large facet on the top is called the table. We'll create each of these sections on a separate layer.

pavilion

crown

table

Draw a Gemstone

To create the pavilion section

① On the **Layers** tab, click on the **Pavilion** layer to make it the active layer. We'll construct the basic outline of the pavilion section of our gemstone.

② On the left Drawing toolbar, on the Quick Shapes flyout, click the ○ **Quick Ellipse**. Hold down the **Ctrl** key and draw a large circle, approximately 10 cm/4 inches in diameter, in the centre of your page.

If required, you can type exact dimensions on the **Transform** tab.

③ On the Quick Shapes flyout, click the ☆ **Quick Star**, then hold down the **Ctrl** key and draw a large star to fill the centre of your circle.

④ With the star selected, drag the node slider at the top of the shape to the right to create an eight-point star.

⑤ Press **Ctrl + A** to select both the circle and the star, and then click the **Align** tab.

⑥ On the **Align** tab, select the **Include Page** check box and then click the **Horizontal Centre** and **Vertical Centre** buttons.

⑦ On the Drawing toolbar, click the ╲ **Straight Line** tool and draw a line from one side of the circle to the other, cutting through the star's points.

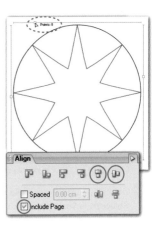

⑧ Repeat the previous step to draw three more lines and complete the shape as illustrated.

⑨ Press **Ctrl + A** to select all the objects, then to the right of the selection, click 🔲 **Group** (or right-click and choose **Group**).

We now need to create separate triangle and diamond shapes that we can fill.

Click the ⊕ **Zoom In** button on the HintLine toolbar to complete the following steps.

10 Click the ✎ **Straight Line** tool, then click a point where one of the line segments meets the outer edge of the circle (**Figure 1**, below).

11 Drag to trace the line down and click at the point where it meets the star shape (**Figure 2**). We've used a red line to illustrate the line tracing.

Drag back up to the circle's edge and click again. Close the shape by clicking again on the first node you created (**Figure 3**).

Finally, click the ▷ **Node** tool and then drag the top line so that it fits the curve of the circle's edge (**Figure 4**).

> 💡 Make sure that you have closed the shape by clicking back on the first node. If you have done so, you'll be able to apply a fill to the new shape created.

| Figure 1 | Figure 2 | Figure 3 | Figure 4 |

12 Select the triangle and press **Ctrl + C** to copy it to the Clipboard.

- Press **Ctrl + V** to paste a copy onto the page.
- On the Standard toolbar, click ⚠ **Flip Horizontal** to create a mirror image of your original triangle.
- Rotate and move the copy into position next to the original, then select both shapes and click ⊞ **Group**.

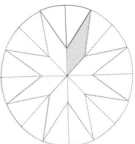

13 Copy the new group and paste it 7 times. Move the groups into position around the edge of the pavilion shape (illustrated in red).

14 Repeat steps 10 to 13 to create the diamond shapes (shaded in blue). When you have finished, you should have a total of 16 triangles and 8 diamonds.

Well done, you've completed the first section of your gemstone! (If you check on the **Layers** tab, you'll see all of your objects displayed in the tree hierarchy, under **Pavilion**.)

In the following section we'll create the gem's crown, and give you another chance to practise your skills with the **Line** and **Node** tools.

Draw a Gemstone

To create the Crown section

1 On the **Layers** tab, click on the **Crown** layer to make it the active layer.

> When you first activate the **Crown** layer, you will still be able to see the shapes you created on the **Pavilion** layer. However, if you try clicking on them, you'll notice that you can't select these objects.
>
> This is precisely why we're using separate layers in our document—the pavilion section we so carefully created is now safe on its own layer and we won't disturb it while we're working on the other layers.

2 On the Quick Shapes flyout, click the ○ **Quick Ellipse**, then hold down the **Ctrl** key and draw a circle exactly the same size as the one on your pavilion layer. You can check the exact dimensions on the **Transform** tab. Position the circle directly on top of the pavilion shape.

3 With the circle selected, in the upper left corner of the **Colour** tab click the **Fill** button and then click the small grey and white swatch to the left of it. This removes the fill from the circle, allowing you to see the objects on the **Pavilion** layer beneath it.

Now that we have the outline for our crown, let's hide the **Pavilion** layer so we're not distracted by it.

4 On the **Layers** tab, click the **Pavilion** layer's 👁 **Hide/Display Layer** button.

Your page now displays only the circle you just created on the **Crown** layer.

5 On the Quick Shapes flyout, click the □ **Quick Rectangle**, then hold down the **Ctrl** key and draw a square, approximately 5 cm/2 inches in size, in the centre of your circle.

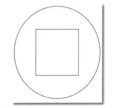

6 Press **Ctrl + A** to select both objects, then on the **Align** tab, click 🗗 **Horizontal Centre** and 🗗 **Vertical Centre**.

7 Right-click the square and click **Copy**, then press **Ctrl + A** to select both items.

On the **Arrange** menu, select **Rotate**, then click **45°**.

8 Right-click on your page and click **Paste**. A second square is pasted into the centre of your circle.

9 Click on the vertical ruler running down the left of your page and drag to position a vertical guideline so that it intersects the corners of one of the squares. Repeat the process on the horizontal ruler to create a horizontal guideline.

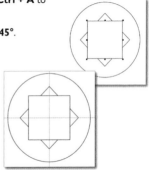

Draw a Gemstone

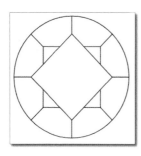

10 Click the ◥ **Straight Line** tool and use the ruler guides to help you draw lines from each corner of the square out to the circle's border.

11 Select all the items on your page again (press **Ctrl + A**, or draw a rectangular selection box around all the items), then click **Arrange/Rotate/45°**.

12 Repeat step 10 to connect the corners of the second square to the circle's edge.

You can remove the ruler guides now if you wish. To do this, just click on the guide and drag it back to the ruler.

13 On the Quick Shapes flyout, click the **Quick Polygon** and draw a polygon on your page, outside of your circle (no need to hold the **Ctrl** key this time).

Drag the shape's upper node handle to the left to create a triangle.

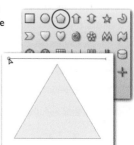

14 Click the ▶ **Pointer** tool, then click on the triangle and drag it to a corner of one of your squares.

15 Resize and rotate the triangle so that its base sits between the corners of the two squares, and its apex extends towards the edge of the circle. (Using the **Pointer** tool, you can click just outside the shape to temporarily switch to the Rotate cursor.)

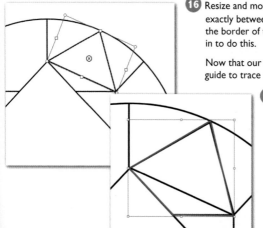

16 Resize and move the triangle so that it fits exactly between the corners of the squares and the border of the circle. You may need to zoom in to do this.

Now that our triangle is in place, let's use it as a guide to trace the outline of the facet.

17 Click the ◥ **Straight Line** tool and trace around the diamond shape that is formed by the top two sides of the triangle and the two edges of the squares.

Do not trace around the base of the triangle. (We've used a red line for illustration purposes.)

Draw a Gemstone

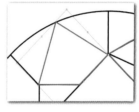

18 Copy and paste the new diamond shape, then use the method described in step 15 or the **Rotate** tool to move the shape into place in the next section of the circle, as illustrated.

19 Repeat the previous step to position six more diamond shapes.

20 Use the methods described in the previous section to create the remaining shapes—you should have 16 triangles around the outer edge of the circle; 8 small triangles around the central octagon shape; and the octagon itself.

21 Before moving on to the final layer, right-click the central octagon shape and click **Copy**.

To create the Table section

1 On the **Layers** tab, click on the **Table** layer to make it the active layer. Now hide the **Crown** layer by clicking the 👁 **Hide/Display Layer** button.

Your page should now appear blank.

2 On the **Edit** menu, click **Paste** to paste a copy of the octagon from your **Crown** layer on to your page.

3 On the **Layers** tab, display all the layers in your drawing by clicking the **Hide/Display Layer** button for the **Crown** and **Pavilion** layers. You should see something that resembles our illustration.

4 At this stage, you might want to save your drawing as a template—click **File/Save As** and save the file as **GemTemplate.dpp**. You can use this template later to create different coloured gems.

Next, we'll create a custom gradient fill to apply colour to our gemstone. We'll show you how to save your fill so that you can use it in future DrawPlus creations.

To apply and create a custom gradient fill

1 If you created a template file, close it now and reopen your original **Gem.dpp** file. We'll start by applying gradient fills to the pavilion of our gemstone, so make the **Pavilion** layer visible and the active layer, and hide the **Crown** and **Table** layers.

2 Select one of the shapes on the pavilion (you can use the ↖ **Pointer** tool or click a shape's thumbnail on the **Layers** tab).

3 On the **Swatches** tab, click the 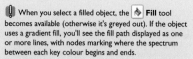 **Gradient** button, select the **Linear** category, and then click on any of the gradient fill swatches.

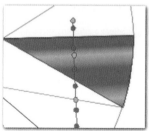

4 On the Drawing toolbar, click the ◈ **Fill** tool. You'll now be able to see the fill path and its nodes.

> 🔲 When you select a filled object, the ◈ **Fill** tool becomes available (otherwise it's greyed out). If the object uses a gradient fill, you'll see the fill path displayed as one or more lines, with nodes marking where the spectrum between each key colour begins and ends.
>
> Adjusting the node positions determines the actual spread of colours between nodes. You can also edit the fill by adding, deleting, or changing key colours. For more information, see online Help.

We want our gemstone to appear iridescent, so we'll edit the fill path and add colours that will create this effect.

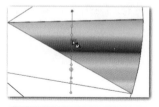

5 On the **Swatches** tab, click on a colour swatch, and then drag over to a node on the fill path to replace the colour.

6 Repeat the previous step, dragging a selection of colours to the fill path until your fill looks something like ours.

In addition to replacing colours on the fill path, you may also want to add some new colour nodes. To do this, simply drag from a colour swatch to a portion of the fill path where there is no node. A new node appears.

> 💡 Be sure the tip of the pointer is over the node or path (watch the cursor) when you release the mouse button. Otherwise the colour will be applied to the whole object as a solid fill.

Let's now save this fill so we can apply it to other facets of the gemstone.

7 To save the fill, right-click, choose **Add to Studio**, then choose **Fill**. In the **Add Fill To Gallery** dialog, give your fill a name and click **OK**.

On the **Swatches** tab, scroll down to see the swatch for your new custom gradient fill.

Draw a Gemstone

8 Click the ↖ **Pointer** tool and select the shape you just filled. On the **Line** tab, remove the outline of the shape by selecting **None** from the line style drop-down list.

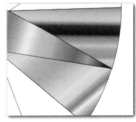

9 Select a different shape and fill it with any linear fill. Repeat steps 5 to 8 to create and apply another custom fill and remove the outline.

10 Repeat the previous steps to create a selection of custom fills for your gemstone's facets.

Make sure you vary the colours and the gradient of the fill path.

> 💡 If you don't want to create your own fills, you can copy ours from the **Gem.dpp** sample file. On the **stages of design layer**, right-click the fills we created and add them to your gallery.

When you've applied your custom fills to all of the facets on the pavilion, it should resemble our illustration, left.

Let's now move on to the **Crown** layer...

To complete the gemstone crown

1 Hide the **Pavilion** layer and make the **Crown** layer visible and the active layer.

2 Apply your custom fills to the shapes on the crown and remove their outlines.

3 Draw a selection bounding box around the entire group of shapes (or press **Ctrl + A**), then on the **Transparency** tab, click the 50% opacity swatch.

4 On the **Layers** tab, make the **Pavilion** layer visible.

You will now be able to see the pavilion through the semi-transparent crown.

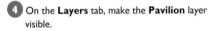

Draw a Gemstone

Almost done! Let's move on and complete the table facet. Here, we'll simply be applying a gradient transparency to a white fill

To complete the gemstone table and apply a gradient transparency

1 Make the **Table** layer visible and the active layer.

2 Apply a solid white fill to the shape and remove its outline.

3 With the octagon selected, on the Drawing toolbar, click the **Transparency** tool and draw a path from the edge of the octagon towards its centre.

You'll see that the shape becomes increasingly opaque as you move the node further towards the opposite side of the octagon.

4 When you're happy with the transparency effect, deselect the **Transparency** tool by clicking the **Pointer** tool.

You'll be glad to know that all the hard work is done and your gemstone is complete. Before we add the finishing touch, here's one last tip that you might find useful.

If your tracing skills are less than perfect, it's likely that some of your shapes and lines extend beyond the border of your circle. Don't worry, you can easily correct this by clipping your image.

To clip an object

1 On the **Layers** tab, make sure all your layers are visible and editable (click the **Edit All Layers** button).

2 Select everything on the page (press **Ctrl + A**, or click **Edit/Select All**), right-click, and then click **Group**.

3 Click the **Quick Ellipse**, hold down the **Ctrl** key and draw a circle exactly the same size as your gemstone.

4 Position this new shape directly on top of your image.

5 Press **Ctrl + A** to select both the gemstone and the circle, then on the **Crop/Uncrop** drop-down menu, click **Clip to Top**.

Draw a Gemstone

Your gemstone is now a perfect circle. You can make it look even more realistic by adding a drop shadow effect.

To create a drop shadow

1. Make the **Crown** layer the active layer. Press **Ctrl + A** to select everything on the page and then click the ⊞ **Group** button, or right-click and choose **Group**.

2. Right-click again and choose **Filter Effects**. In the **Filter Effects** dialog, select the **Drop Shadow** check box and set the following values:

- **Opacity:** 30
- **Blur:** 50
- **Intensity:** 4
- **Lock:** Bottom
- **Scale Y:** 35

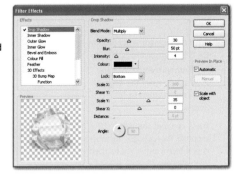

(You can also use the ⬛ **Shadow** tool to create and edit a drop-shadow 'on the page.')

Congratulations! You've created a gemstone from scratch. We've covered a lot of ground in this tutorial, and you should now be feeling more familiar with some of DrawPlus's powerful tools and features. We hope that you have enjoyed the exercise, and have learned a few things in the process.

If you're feeling adventurous, open your **GemTemplate.dpp** file, save it with a different file name, and then try creating coloured gemstones by applying different linear fills. Or why not experiment with different shaped gemstones...

💡 If you want to create a single-colour gemstone that you can quickly recolour, we suggest you use **linked colours**.

For more information, see the "Create a Velvet Effect" Level 1 tutorial or online Help.

Make a Clock Face

In this tutorial, we'll show you how to draw a clock face from scratch, creating the various elements on separate layers. We'll also teach you a quick and easy way to position objects around a circle using grouping and rotation.

You'll learn how to:

- Use the **Layers** tab to add new layers and to hide and display layers.

- Use Quick Shapes and lines to create custom shapes.

- Apply filter effects.

- Group, rotate, and crop objects.

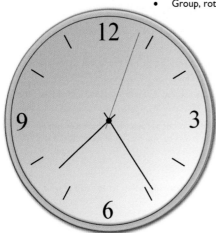

Make a Clock Face

To begin, we'll give you a brief introduction to layers. We recommend you read the following section before beginning to draw.

Introducing layers

By default, all new DrawPlus documents consist of a single layer. Objects created on this layer are stacked in order, from back to front, with each new object in front of the others.

> 💡 For simple designs, one layer is usually sufficient. If you're working on a complex design, however, it makes sense to separate groups of objects on different layers. This allows you to work on one layer at a time without disturbing elements on other layers.

At the right of the DrawPlus workspace you'll see the **Layers** tab, which displays all the layers in a document and their properties (you can turn these on or off by clicking the appropriate button). The hierarchical tree view displays thumbnail previews of the objects on each layer.

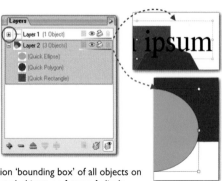

- To display the objects contained on a layer, click the + sign to the left of the layer to expand it.

- To see a larger preview of an object, hover over a thumbnail preview.

- To select an object on the page, click it's thumbnail.

- The coloured line under each layer's properties buttons indicates the colour of the selection 'bounding box' of all objects on this layer. In our illustration, selected objects on **Layer 1** display with a blue selection bounding box; objects on **Layer 2** display with a red bounding box.

- Use the buttons at the bottom of the **Layers** tab to add and delete layers, change the layer order, edit all, and/or view all layers.

We'll be using some of these buttons in this tutorial. For more detailed information, see online Help.

Although the clock face we're going to create is not particularly complicated, we'll construct its various elements on separate layers so you can see the benefits of this approach. Let's begin...

To create a document and add layers

1 In the DrawPlus Startup Wizard, choose **Drawing**, select a page size of your choice and click **Open**.

2 On the **Layers** tab, right-click the layer name— **Layer 1**—and select **Layer Properties**. In the **Layer Properties** dialog, in the **Name:** box, type 'Border' and click **OK**.

3 On the **Layers** tab, click the ✚ **Add Layer** button. Name this second layer 'Background' and click **OK**.

4 Repeat the previous step to add two more layers named 'Minutes' and 'Hands.'

To create the Background layer graphics

1 On the **Layers** tab, click the **Background** layer to make it the active layer.

2 On the Drawing toolbar, on the Quick Shapes flyout, click the ⬭ **Quick Ellipse**, then hold down the **Ctrl** key and draw a large circle in the middle of your page. Select the circle.

3 On the **Swatches** tab, click the 🎨▾ **Palettes** drop-down list and choose the **Standard RGB** palette. Click on a mid-grey swatch (we used **RGB(187, 187, 187)**) to apply it to your shape.

4 Click the 🖌 **Fill** tool and drag a fill path diagonally across the shape.

5 Drag the ends of the fill path to create a subtle gradient fill, as illustrated.

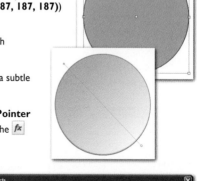

6 On the Drawing toolbar, click the ⬏ **Pointer** tool to select the circle and then click the *fx* **Filter Effects** button.

7 In the **Filter Effects** dialog, select the **Inner Shadow** check box and set the following values:

- **Opacity:** 35
- **Blur:** 3.8
- **Lock:** Centre
- **Distance:** 5
- **Angle:** 90
- Click **OK**.

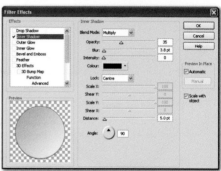

Make a Clock Face

8 With the circle selected, on the **Align** tab, click **Horizontal Centre** and **Vertical Centre**.

You've completed the first layer of your clock face.

(You'll see your shape displayed in the tree hierarchy on the **Layers** tab.)

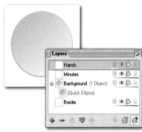

Let's move on and create the clock's border.

To create the Border layer graphics

1 With the circle selected, on the **Tools** menu, click **Transform**.

In the **Transform** dialog, set the **Scale** value to **110%** and click **OK**.

DrawPlus pastes a 10% larger copy of the circle directly on top of the original, and selects it.

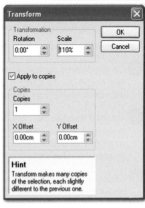

2 Press **Ctrl + X** to copy this new shape to the Clipboard and cut it from the **Background** layer.

3 On the **Layers** tab, click the **Border** layer to make it the active layer.

4 Press **Ctrl + V** to paste the copied shape back into the document, but this time onto the **Background** layer.

5 On the **Swatches** tab, apply a mid-grey solid fill. Leave the outline black.

6 Right-click the circle and on the Drawing toolbar, click **Filter Effects**. In the **Filter Effects** dialog, select the **Inner Glow** check box and set the following values:

- **Opacity:** 75
- **Blur:** 25
- **Intensity:** 14
- **Colour:** Choose a mid-grey swatch

Now select the **Bevel and Emboss** check box and in the **Style** drop-down list, select **Pillow Emboss**.

- Click **OK**.

With the background and border of the clock complete, we'll now create the numbers and five-minute markings and position them around the edge of the clock. Don't worry, you won't have to position each one by hand, we'll create the first one and then let DrawPlus do the difficult part for us.

To create the clock numbers and five-minute markings

1 On the **Layers** tab, click the **Minutes** layer to make it the active layer.

2 On the Drawing toolbar, click the **Λ Text** tool, then click on your page and type the number '12.'

3 Click the **Pointer** tool and then select the text object .

On the Text context toolbar, select the font style and size that you want to use for your clock numbers—we've used **48 pt Times New Roman**.

4 Drag the number into position on the clock face. With the number still selected, click the **Align** tab and then click the **Horizontal Centre** button.

> Because the text object is the only object selected, DrawPlus will align it relative to the page edges.

5 Repeat steps 2 to 4 to create and position the number 6.

6 Repeat steps 2 to 4 to create and position the numbers 3 and 9.

This time, on the **Align** tab, click **Vertical Centre.**

Our next task is to create the five-minute markings between our numbers. We'll use the **Straight Line** tool to create the first one, then we'll make use of DrawPlus's 'copy and paste,' and rotation functionality to create and position the others.

Make a Clock Face

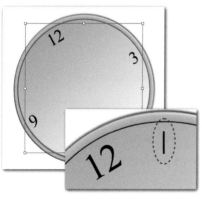

7 Draw a selection bounding box around all four of the numbers, then on the **Arrange** menu, point to **Rotate** and click **30°**.

Your clock face should now look like our illustration, left.

8 On the Drawing toolbar, click the **Straight Line** tool, then click on your clock face and draw a vertical line in the upper centre of your clock face.

9 With the line selected, on the **Line** tab, adjust the thickness of the line by dragging the slider, or by selecting a value from the drop-down list.

Your line can be any length and thickness you like, depending on the size you chose to make your numbers. (Ours is approximately 1 cm long and 2 pts thick.)

10 Use the **Align** tab to centre the line horizontally.

11 With the line still selected, click **Edit**, then **Copy** (or press **Ctrl + C**) to place a copy on the Clipboard.

12 Select all the objects on the **Minutes** layer (draw a selection bounding box around them, or press **Ctrl + A**) then on the **Arrange** menu, point to **Rotate** and click **30°**.

13 Click anywhere on the page to clear your selection, then on the **Edit** menu, click **Paste** (or press **Ctrl + V**). A copy of your line is pasted back on to the clock face in the original position.

14 Repeat step 12, this time choosing a rotation of **60°** (so that you skip over the number 9).

15 Repeat step 13 to paste the next line in place.

16 Repeat the rotation and pasting process until you have placed all eight markings on your clock face.

17 Press **Ctrl + A** to select all the numbers and lines, then to the lower right of the selection, click **Group** (or right-click and choose **Group**).

Make a Clock Face

With all our numbers and five-minute markings in place, it's time to move on to the final element of the clock face—the hands.

To create the clock hands

1 On the **Layers** tab, click the **Hands** layer to make it the active layer.

2 On the Drawing toolbar, on the Quick Shapes flyout, click the ⃝ **Quick Ellipse**, then hold down the **Ctrl** key and draw a small circle in the middle of your clock face. Apply a solid black fill and outline.

3 Use the **Align** tab to centre the shape horizontally and vertically.

4 On the Drawing toolbar, click the ╲ **Straight Line** tool and create the minutes hand by drawing a line from the outer edge of the clock face through the centre circle.

5 Repeat step 4 to create the hours hand. Make this line a little shorter.

6 Select both lines (select one line, then press and hold the **Shift** key and click the second line), then on the **Line** tab, increase the line thickness to 2.0 pts.

7 Draw a third line for the seconds hand and decrease the thickness to 0.5 pt.

8 Again, if you want to, you can select all the objects on this layer and group them.

And that's all there is to it! You've created a simple clock with all of its groups of elements on different layers.

> You'll find our example—**Clock Face.dpp**—in the **Workspace** folder of your DrawPlus installation directory—normally located at:
>
> **C:\Program Files\Serif\DrawPlus\X2\ Tutorials\Workspace**

Make a Clock Face

Designing with layers provides you with a great deal of flexibility. You can play around with objects on a particular layer, hide layers, create new objects on new layers, and so on, without interfering with your basic design.

For example, you might want to hide the **Minutes** layer, and create an alternative layer (Minutes 2) on which you have numbers instead of five-minute markings. (Note that if you do add new layers, you'll probably have to reorder them on the **Layers** tab.)

You could also experiment with different fills and filter effects, or even import a photograph into your **Background** layer and then crop it to create a personalized clock face.

💡 If you're feeling adventurous, here's a simple and inexpensive way to create unique gifts for friends and family...

Many of the basic clocks you can buy today can be taken apart, allowing you to pop off the hands and replace the faceplate with your own personalized design or photograph.

Simply create your background design in DrawPlus, making sure your circle matches the exact measurement of your clock's faceplate, and then snap everything back together!

Make a Family Tree

On the DrawPlus **Gallery** tab, you'll find an extensive collection of predefined objects—symbols, shape art, text art, logos, and so on—that you can use in your drawings. The various objects are divided into categories, which are displayed in a drop-down list at the top of the **Gallery** tab.

In this tutorial, we'll introduce you to the Gallery's **Family Tree** category.

You'll learn how to:

- Place symbols from the Gallery on to your page.

- Group, ungroup, and align objects.

- Use the **Connector** tool.

- Import, resize, and crop photographs.

- Make adjustments to image brightness and contrast, and enhance vintage photographs.

- Edit and format text objects.

- Add a background texture.

Make a Family Tree

- In the DrawPlus Startup Wizard, choose **Drawing**, select a 'Portrait' page size of your choice and click **Open**.

To create the tree structure

1 On the right of the workspace, click the **Gallery** tab, and then in the category drop-down list expand the **Connecting Symbols/Family Tree/Photographic** category to display the various symbols available.

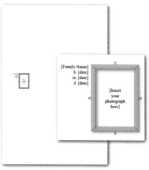

Click on the **Single Photo Frame** symbol, drag it over to the left side of your page and then release the mouse button.

2 Select the text box inside the photo frame and press the **Delete** key.

3 Select the frame and remaining text box by drawing a selection bounding box around them. Click the ▦ **Group** button below the selection.

💡 When objects are grouped, you can move, resize, rotate, or shear them all at the same time.

4 On the **Align** tab, click ▦ **Vertical Centre**.

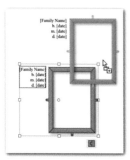

5 With the frame and text box group still selected, press and hold the **Ctrl** key and then drag away to create a copy of the group.

6 Position the copied group above and to the right of the original group.

7 With the new copy still selected, hold down the **Ctrl** key and then drag another copy down, keeping it vertically aligned with the second group by holding down the **Shift** key.

If you need to adjust the position of your groups, you can align them at any stage by using the **Align** tab.

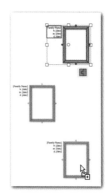

8 Repeat the **Ctrl** + drag procedure to create and position an additional 12 photo frame objects.

Your finished structure should resemble our illustration, right.

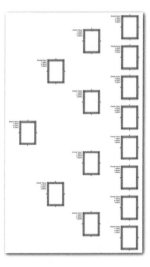

💡 To space objects evenly on a page, vertically or horizontally, select all the objects and then in the **Align Objects** dialog, select the **Space Evenly** option.

Our next task is to connect the photo frames. We'll use the **Connector** tool to do this, but before we do so, we need to break up the photo frame and text box groups (remember we grouped them earlier in step 3).

9 To ungroup, select any frame and text box object then click 🔲 **Ungroup**. Repeat this step for each frame group.

10 On the Drawing toolbar, on the Line tools flyout, click the 🔩 **Connector** tool. On the context toolbar, the Connector controls and buttons are now displayed.

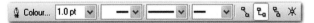

11 On the context toolbar, click the 🔩 **Right Angle Connector** tool.

Hover the cursor over a frame to display its **connection points**.

These default connection points can't be moved or deleted, but you can create additional ones if required. For more information, see online Help.

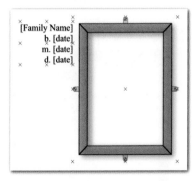

Make a Family Tree

12 Starting with the leftmost photo frame, click on its upper connection point and then drag to the left connection point of the frame above it.

Repeat this procedure to connect each photo frame to each of its two 'parent' frames.

Your finished structure should resemble ours.

Congratulations! You've completed the basic 'tree' structure of your family tree. Now it's time to add the photographs and personal details for each of your family members.

To import and crop a photograph

1 On the Drawing toolbar, click the 🖼 **Insert Picture** button.

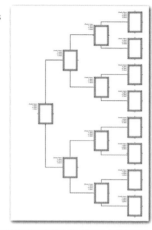

In the **Insert Picture** dialog, browse to locate the photograph you want to import, click to select the file, and then click **Open**.

The dialog disappears and the mouse pointer changes to the 🖼 **Picture Import** cursor.

What you do next determines the initial size, placement, and aspect ratio (proportions) of the image.

- To insert the picture at a default size, simply click the mouse.

- or -

- To set the size of the inserted picture, drag out a region and release the mouse button. Normally, the picture's aspect ratio is preserved.

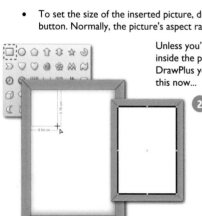

Unless you're lucky, your photograph won't fit exactly inside the photo frame. Don't worry though, with DrawPlus you can crop an image to any size. Let's do this now...

2 On the Drawing toolbar, on the **Quick Shapes** flyout, choose the ☐ **Quick Rectangle**.

Click in the upper left corner of a photo frame, and then drag out a rectangle to fit inside the frame.

3 On the **Colour** tab, click the small **No Fill** button to make the shape transparent.

4 Drag the rectangle into position on top of your photograph.

5 Now select both the photograph and the **Quick Rectangle**.

On the Standard toolbar, in the **Crop** drop-down list, click **Crop to Top**.

6 Now drag your photo inside its photo frame—it should fit perfectly.

Now that you've imported your first photo, you can repeat these steps to add the rest of your family photos to your family tree.

If you're working with old or less-than-perfect photos, you might want to improve the image quality, or apply a similar style to all of the photos.

DrawPlus includes some powerful image adjustment tools that enable you to adjust images after importing them.

To learn more, see page 177, "Making image adjustments."

> Note that any image adjustments must be made before cropping your photographs.

If you are happy with the quality of your imported photographs, however, you can move right on to the next section.

Make a Family Tree

With all your photos in place, it's time to put your family members' details into the text boxes. The photo frame template we are using in this exercise provides placeholders for family name, date of birth, marriage, and death, but you can add any information you want.

[Family Name]
b. [date]
m. [date]
d. [date]

To add family member details

1 With the ![Pointer icon] **Pointer** tool, click any text box to select it. On the Text context toolbar, select the font size and style you want to use.

Times New Roman ▼ | 6.0 pt ▼ | **B** *I* <u>U</u> | ≣ ≣ ≣ ≣

2 On the HintLine toolbar, click ⊕ **Zoom In** to zoom into the area you're working on.

3 Click the **Λ Artistic Text** tool, then click and drag to select all of the text inside the text box.

Replace the placeholder text with your family member's details.

Well done, you've completed your family tree!

At this point, you could simply add a title to your masterpiece (using the **Λ Artistic Text** tool), and then print it out.

However, if you'd like to add some creative flair and interest to your family tree, we've got a few ideas to inspire you...

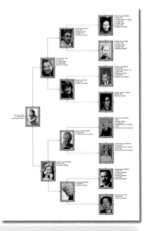

Robert Charles DAVIES
b. 2 Sept 1915
in Croydon, Surrey, England
m. 10 Jun 1945
in Cardiff, Wales
d. 22 Dec 2003
in Brighton, England

💧 Note that in our family tree we added the place of birth, marriage, and death (where applicable).

We also moved the text boxes to the right of the photo frames, and changed the text alignment by selecting each text box and then clicking the **Align Left** button on the Text context toolbar.

Example 1: Applying an effect from the Effects tab

DrawPlus provides you with a wide range of preset effects that you can apply to any filled shape, including text. Once you've applied an effect, you can customize it and then add it to the **Effects** tab—making it available to use again. For more information, see online Help.

To apply an effect

1 Draw a ☐ **Quick Rectangle** the size of the page and place it behind your family tree structure by clicking **Arrange/Order Objects/Send to Back**. On the **Colour** tab, apply any colour fill to the shape.

2 With the rectangle selected, click the **Effects** tab and choose **Wood** from the drop-down category list. Click the **Basswood** thumbnail to apply it.

3 On the **Transparency** tab, click a swatch to apply the desired opacity value.

Example 2: Applying a paper texture

With DrawPlus paper textures you can quickly and easily add an interesting textured background to your creations. Here's how we did it...

To apply a paper texture

1 Draw a ☐ **Quick Rectangle** the size of your page and place it behind the family tree structure.

2 With the shape selected, on the **Swatches** tab apply a mid pink colour—we used RGB(255, 218, 218).

3 On the **Layers** tab, click the ■ **Apply Paper Texture** button.

4 In the **Bitmap Selector** dialog, choose the **Abstract** category, click the **Bitmap Swatches 4** swatch, and then click **OK** to apply it to the page.

Make a Family Tree

Example 3: Creating a background image

For something really unique, why not add a watermark effect to your family tree. You can use any image or photograph for this, and the process is very simple.

In our example, we used a photograph of a tree. Equally effective would be an image that holds some special significance for your family. The following steps explain how we achieved this effect by creating a new layer in our document.

To create a background image

1. On the **Layers** tab, click the ✥ **Add Layer** button. The new layer (Layer 2) displays at the top of the **Layers** tab list and is selected by default.

2. With the new layer still selected, on the **Layers** tab click the ➡ **Move Layer Down** button. This places Layer 2 behind Layer 1 in your document.

Let's temporarily hide Layer 1 so that we can concentrate on our Layer 2 image.

3. On the **Layers** tab, click the 👁 **Hide/Show Layer** button for Layer 1.

   Your family tree disappears (don't worry, it's only temporary—click the **Hide/Show Layer** button again if you don't believe us!), leaving you with a blank page displayed.

4. Click the 🖼 **Insert Picture** button and import your image, resizing it so that it fills your page.

5. With the image selected, on the **Transparency** tab, apply 26% opacity.

6. Finally, click the **Hide/Show Layer** button to display Layer 1 on top of Layer 2.

💡 Try creating a range of different background images and textures, each on different layers. You can then experiment with various effects by displaying different combinations of layers.

Making image adjustments

In the next section we'll demonstrate how to use the new **Image Adjustments** dialog to enhance your images. Keep in mind, however, that because all photographs are unique, you may have to experiment with various adjustments and settings to achieve results you are happy with.

Correcting bright and dark photographs

Too bright or too dark photographs are fairly common, so this adjustment is one you'll probably end up using quite often.

To adjust image brightness and contrast

1 Import the required image. Notice that the **Picture context toolbar** displays.

2 With the image selected, click the **Image Adjustments** button.

3 In the **Image Adjustments** dialog, click the **Add Adjustment** button and then select **Brightness and Contrast**.

4 Adjust the image brightness and contrast by dragging the sliders.

The **Image Preview** pane updates to show the effects of your adjustments.

When you are happy with your results, click **OK**.

If you're importing a number of photos, you can use the image adjustment tools to give them all a consistent look and feel.

In this example we applied a Diffuse Glow effect to create a soft dream-like quality.

Make a Family Tree

Enhancing vintage photographs

For our family tree example, we imported a number of vintage photographs. Old photos tend to vary greatly in quality and this is one area in which you'll need to experiment with the various image adjustment tools. Bear in mind that you will only achieve a certain level of improvement—you will not get a perfect finished result, but you should be able to enhance the image significantly. The following steps describe how we enhanced one of our photos.

> You can use the Picture context toolbar for some image adjustments—applying transparency, adjusting brightness and contrast, adjusting levels, and fixing red eye.

To enhance a vintage photograph

1. Import the required image and with the image selected, click the **Image Adjustments** button.

2. In the **Image Adjustments** dialog, click the **Add Adjustment** button and then select **Brightness and Contrast**.

   Adjust the image brightness and contrast by dragging the sliders or typing directly into the boxes. (We reduced brightness and increased contrast.)

3. Click the **Add Adjustment** button again and select **Hue/Saturation/Lightness**.

   Adjust the values. (We increased hue and reduced saturation.)

4. Experiment with the other adjustments and when you are happy with your results, click **OK** to apply them.

> The DrawPlus image adjustment tools provide you with the means to enhance your images and correct minor imperfections.
>
> However, to correct more severe flaws—rips, scratches, and so on—you'll need to use photo-editing software such as Serif PhotoPlus.

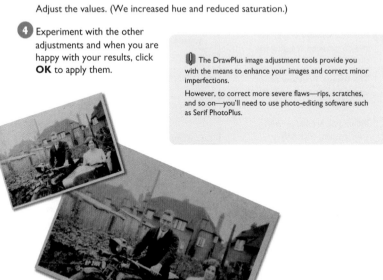

Design a Cartoon Movie Poster

The poster—the oldest medium of all—has become an integral part of our society. Its functions are many and include publicity, promotion, advertising, communication, selling, as well as decoration.

However, before it can do any of the above, the first objective of any poster is to attract the attention of its audience.

In this tutorial we'll discuss the various elements of poster design—layout, typeface, graphics, and so on, and show you how to combine these elements into an effective layout. You'll learn how to:

- Lay out a poster publication.

- Use colour effectively in a layout.

- Position and align text and graphics objects.

- Use a variety of typefaces to create different effects.

- Adjust letter spacing.

- Apply gradient fills, filter effects, and perspective.

- Draw a cartoon character using basic Quick Shapes.

- Set up page and printer options.

- Use tiling and scaling to print your poster on multiple pages.

Design a Cartoon Movie Poster

For our fictitious movie, 'Catboy,' we wanted to create a crisp, clean cartoon-style poster.

- For maximum visual impact, we chose blue and orange (complementary colours) along with black and white.

- To keep the layout simple, we kept graphics to a minimum and let the text do most of the work.

- The chunky style of the title text is contrasted with the simpler text style used for the copy line and the credits.

- The copy line "Mischief is coming" and the single image of the main character give the audience a clue as to the movie's genre.

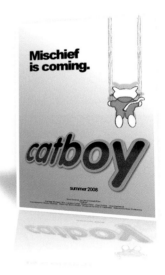

The following pages provide step-by-step instructions to recreate our Catboy poster.

To create the gradient background

1. In the DrawPlus Startup Wizard, choose **Drawing**, select an **A4** or **Letter Portrait** size page and click **Open**.

2. On the Drawing toolbar, on the Quick Shapes flyout, click the ▢ **Quick Rectangle**. Click in the upper left corner of the page, hold down the mouse button and then drag out a large rectangle to almost fill your page. (We left a 0.4 cm border between the rectangle and the page edge.)

3. On the Drawing toolbar click the ◈ **Fill** tool. Click and drag a fill path from the upper right corner to the lower left corner.

4. On the **Swatches** tab, locate a mid blue swatch, then click and drag it over to the black node at the bottom of the fill path.

   (You can also click the node first, and then click the swatch you want to apply.)

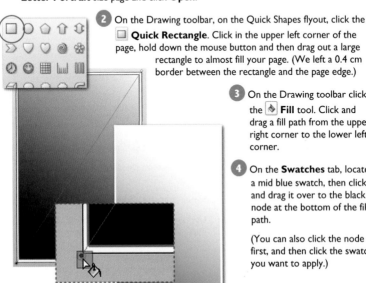

Design a Cartoon Movie Poster

5 Now that we have created the background for our poster, we can create the individual elements to place on it. Let's start with the main element—the movie title.

To create the title text

1 On the Drawing toolbar, click the **Λ Artistic Text** tool, then click anywhere outside the blue rectangle and type the word 'catboy.'

2 Double-click the text to select the whole word.

On the Text context toolbar:

- In the font name drop-down list, select **Elementary Heavy SF**.

- In the font size list, choose **200 pt**.

3 If necessary, use the **Pointer** tool to select your text object and reposition it on the page.

Now for some colour... We'll begin by applying a simple gradient fill to add depth to our title.

4 Select the text object, then click the **Fill** tool and draw a vertical line through the title from top to bottom.

5 On the **Swatches** tab, click a brown swatch (we used **RGB(128, 80, 47)**) and then drag it over to the node at the bottom of the fill path.

Note: We dragged the top node up to reduce the amount of black in the text fill.

6 Click the **Pointer** tool and then click the text object. On the **Swatches** tab, click the **Line** button and then click an orange swatch.

7 On the **Line** tab, select a solid line and increase the line thickness to 7.5 pt.

Our title is starting to come together, but there are still a few things we can do to improve it. Next, we'll reduce the letter spacing.

8 With the text object selected, click the **Node** tool. Adjustment sliders and handles appear. The rightmost node is the **Letter** slider, click and drag this node to the left until the letters of the title touch.

Design a Cartoon Movie Poster

You'll notice that some of the letters overlap a little too much. Don't worry, we can easily correct this by adjusting the 'offset'—the spacing of individual letters.

9 Click on the node to the left of the letter 't,' then drag it slightly to the right until the 'a' and 't' just touch.

10 Repeat this step to adjust the remaining letters.

Let's now add the final touches—perspective and filter effects.

11 With the text object selected, on the Drawing toolbar, click the 🖻 **Perspective** tool. The Ⓐ **Node** tool becomes the active tool and an adjustment slider appears above the object.

- Click and drag directly on the text with the **Node** tool, which displays a 3D cursor.

- or -

- Drag the adjustment slider to customize the effect.

12 On the Drawing toolbar, click *fx* **Filter Effects**. In the **Filter Effects** dialog, select the **Drop Shadow** check box and set the following values:

- **Opacity:** 50

- **Blur:** 6

- **Distance:** 1.5

- **Angle:** 120

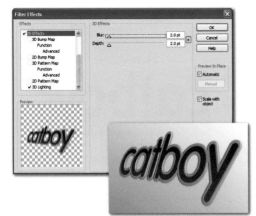

13 In the **Filter Effects** dialog, select the **3D Effects** check box and set both the **Blur** and **Depth** values to 2 pt.

14 Finally, select the **3D Lighting** check box and then click **OK** to close the dialog and apply the filter effects.

Congratulations—your movie title is complete!

Let's now move on and create the star of the show—the one and only Catboy!

Design a Cartoon Movie Poster

You don't need to be an artist to create our cartoon character—you'll be pleased to know that he is very easily constructed from a few basic Quick Shapes.

To draw Catboy

1 On the Drawing toolbar, on the Quick Shapes flyout, click the ○ **Quick Ellipse** and draw a wide flattened ellipse for the basic head shape.

2 Repeat the process to draw a small elongated ear shape.

3 Select the small shape and then click the ✿ **Rotate** tool. Now click on one of the shape's corner handles and rotate the shape approximately 45° to the right.

4 With the shape still selected, right-click and choose **Copy**. Then right-click again and choose **Paste**.

A copy of the shape is pasted directly on top of the original and is selected by default.

5 On the Standard toolbar, click the ◢◣ **Flip Horizontal** button to flip the copied shape. Now drag the two shapes into position, as illustrated right.

6 Click the ▶ **Pointer** tool and then draw a selection bounding box around the three ellipses to select them all (or click one shape, then hold down the **Shift** key and click on the others to add them to the selection).

7 On the Standard toolbar, click the 🖻 **Add** button to combine the shapes.

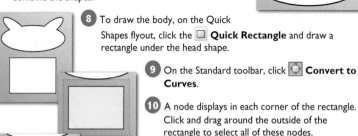

8 To draw the body, on the Quick Shapes flyout, click the ☐ **Quick Rectangle** and draw a rectangle under the head shape.

9 On the Standard toolbar, click ⊙ **Convert to Curves**.

10 A node displays in each corner of the rectangle. Click and drag around the outside of the rectangle to select all of these nodes.

11 On the Curve context bar, click the ⌒ **Smart Corner** button to round the corners of your shape.

Design a Cartoon Movie Poster

12 Repeat step 4 to copy and paste the rounded rectangle. We'll use this shape for Catboy's arm—resize it and move it into place, then repeat the copy and paste process to create the other arm.

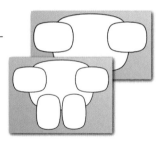

13 Repeat the previous step to create the legs.

14 Select the body, arms, and legs shapes and then click the 🖾 **Add** button to combine them.

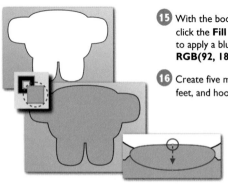

15 With the body selected, on the **Swatches** tab, click the **Fill** button and then click a blue swatch to apply a blue fill to the shape (we used **RGB(92, 188, 252)**).

16 Create five more ellipses for Catboy's hands, feet, and hood.

17 To flatten the top of the hood, convert the shape to curves and then drag the top node down a little, as illustrated.

Next, we'll create the tail with a freeform shape:

18 On the Drawing toolbar, click the ✍ **Freeform Paint** tool.

- On the context toolbar, set the **Width** to 8.
- On the **Swatches** tab, set the **Fill** to white and the outline to black.

Click where you want the shape to start, and hold the mouse button down as you draw.

The shape appears immediately and follows your mouse movements. To complete the shape, release the mouse button.

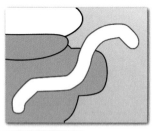

19 Click the ✏ **Pencil** tool use it to draw the whiskers. (Note that you'll have to select the tool each time you want to draw a new line.)

20 Press and hold down the **Alt** key, then use the **Pointer** tool to draw a selection bounding box around Catboy.

To the lower right of the selection, click  **Group**.

> When selecting objects that are positioned on top of another object—in this case the blue gradient background—holding down the **Alt** key allows you begin drawing the selection box over the background object without including it in the multiple selection.

21 On the Drawing toolbar, click *fx* **Filter Effects** (or right-click the Catboy figure and choose **Filter Effects**).

In the **Filter Effects** dialog, select the **Drop Shadow** check box and set the following values:

- **Opacity:** 12
- **Blur:** 3.8
- **Distance:** 19.5
- **Angle:** 270

Click **OK**.

22 That's it, Catboy is complete! Just use the **Pointer** tool to drag him into position.

The remaining elements of the poster are very simple to create. Rather than breaking them down into step-by-step procedures, we'll briefly summarize each element instead. We'll list the tools and settings we used, and point out any specific design considerations where applicable.

> If you want to compare your finished poster with ours, you'll find the sample file—**Catboy.dpp**—in the **Workspace** folder of your DrawPlus installation directory—normally located at:
>
> **C:\Program Files\Serif\DrawPlus\X2\ Tutorials\Workspace**

Design a Cartoon Movie Poster

To create the scratches

1. We first drew a line with the **Pencil** tool and applied a mid-grey colour.

2. With the line selected, we used the **Roughen** tool to create a jagged effect.

3. Once we were happy with our first set of scratches, we grouped them, and then copied and pasted the group to create the second set.

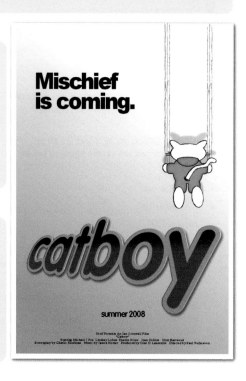

We wanted a clean 'sans serif' font for the copy line and decided on **60 pt Arial Black**.

This font style contrasts sharply with the title text and is a perfect fit for the black-outlined cartoon-style graphic.

The size is big enough to grab attention, but not so big that it overpowers the layout.

We used **21 pt Elementary Heavy** SF for the 'summer 2008' line—here we are continuing a theme by echoing the same font style used in the title text.

The credit lines are in **7 pt Times New Roman**—a traditional serif font. When using small text, it's advisable to use a serif font to maximize readability.

Congratulations! You have finished your poster and are ready to print it out!

In the following section, we'll discuss the various printing options available in DrawPlus.

Note the centre alignment of the credit text lines. This symmetry is a nice contrast to the position of the other elements of our poster.

Printing your poster

Our sample poster was created on a standard A4 paper size. However, posters and banners are often large-format documents where the page size extends across multiple sheets of paper. To have DrawPlus take care of the printing, set up your document beforehand. You can do this in one of the following ways:

- From the DrawPlus Startup Wizard, click **Start New Drawing**, select the **Large Publications** option, then choose from one of the preset templates.

  - or -

- In DrawPlus, click **File** then click **Page Setup**. In the **Page Setup** dialog, choose the **Large** option and select from the drop-down list of templates.

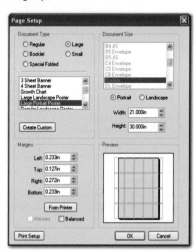

Tiling and scaling

If your document isn't set up as a poster or banner, you can use tiling and scaling settings to print large (or enlarged) pages using multiple sheets of paper. Each section or tile is printed on a single sheet of paper, and the various tiles can then be joined to form the complete page. To simplify arrangement of the tiles and to allow for printer margins, you can specify an overlap value.

To print a poster or banner from a standard page

1 In the **Print** dialog, click the **Layout** tab.

2 On the **Layout** tab:

- In the **Special Printing** section, select the **As in document** option and then set the **% Scale factor**.

- In the **Tiling** section, select the **Print tiled pages** option, and then set the **Tile overlap** required (to allow for printer margins).

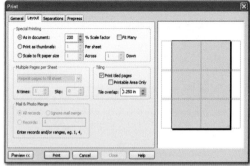

To the right of the **Layout** tab, the preview shows you how many pages will be required to print the document.

Design a Cartoon Movie Poster

Generating professional output

There may be times when you want a professional printer to output your DrawPlus document. For example:

- If you need to reproduce more than about 500 copies (photocopying begins to lose its economic advantages at this point).

- If you need spot colour or process colour printing for a particular job.

    The **Print** dialog's **Prepress** tab allows you set special options such as bleed limit, crop marks, and so on.

    For more information, see the "Setting prepress options" topic in online Help.

PostScript® files

A standard way of delivering a desktop document to a commercial printer or service bureau is to generate one or more **PostScript® files** that can be passed along on disk or via modem to the bureau.

For detailed information and instructions, see the "Generating professional output" topic in online Help.

PDF files

Another option for delivering files to a bureau or commercial printer is Adobe's **Portable Document Format** (PDF). PDF is increasingly used to distribute documents as electronic 'replicas' over the Web. Anyone using Adobe's Acrobat Reader, regardless of their computer platform, can view and/or print out your document in its original form.

For details on exporting your DrawPlus documents to PDF format, see the "Exporting PDF files" topic in online Help.

💡 Why not have your movie poster or cartoon character printed on a novelty item such as a T-shirt, mouse pad. or mug.

With DrawPlus you can export your design to various file formats, such as JPEG or TIFF. You can also change settings such as file size and resolution.

Contact your local print shop to find out the exact file specifications they require to print a particular item.

Design a Garden

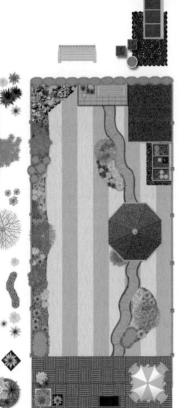

Located on the **Gallery** tab, in the **Layout Symbols** category, you'll find the **Garden** layout symbols.

This extensive image collection includes garden furniture, buildings, surfaces, paths and borders, as well as a selection of containers, bedding plants, trees, and shrubs.

Simply 'drag and drop' your favourite images onto the page to quickly and easily design beautiful garden layouts.

Follow the steps in this tutorial and learn how to:

- Scale your drawing to your garden.

- Use ruler guides to help you position objects on the page.

- Place **Garden** symbols on to your page, resizing them where necessary.

- Align and order objects on the page.

Design a Garden

> You'll find our sample garden layout, **Garden.dpp**, in the **Workspace** folder of your DrawPlus installation directory—normally located at:
> **C:\Program Files\Serif\DrawPlus\X2\Tutorials\Workspace**

Our garden is 6 metres wide by 13 metres long. At the moment, the whole area is grass, but we have big plans! We want to keep a big expanse of lawn; however, we also want to build a summerhouse and a deck/patio area for outdoor eating. We'd love a cold frame, and really need a shed to store bikes and gardening tools. Trouble is, we can't decide where all of these elements should go. Fortunately, we've got DrawPlus to help us out!

Let's start by creating our document and setting up the scale options.

To scale a drawing

① In the DrawPlus Startup Wizard, choose **Drawing**. Select a Letter or A4 Portrait page size and click **Open**.

Before we begin to design, we need to decide what scale factor to use to fit our garden on to the page. If we set one metre of garden space to equal two centimetres, we can represent our 6 m by 13 m garden in a 12 cm by 26 cm page area.

② On the **Tools** menu, click **Options**.

③ In the **Options** dialog, select the **Drawing Scale** option.

- Select the **Scale Drawing** check box.

- Under **Page Distance:** Enter '2,' and select 'centimetres' as the page unit.

- Under **Ruler Distance:** Enter '1,' and select 'metres' as the ruler unit.

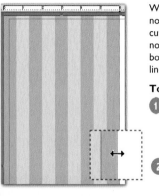

With our page set up to scale we can place our lawn section.

When you design your garden, remember that your drawing will not print right to the edge of the page. To avoid having the printer cut off the edges of the lawn, we need to make sure that it does not extend into the page margins (represented by solid blue lines bordering the page). We'll use ruler guides—non-printing, red lines—to help us position our lawn appropriately.

To position the lawn using ruler guides

① On the **Gallery** tab, in the category drop-down list, click **Layout Symbols**. Expand the **Garden** category and click **Surfaces and Features**. Scroll down the list of symbols and find **Lawn 9**. Click and drag it over to your page.

② Resize the lawn to 6 m by 13 m by dragging the size handles.

Design a Garden

3 To create a vertical ruler guide, click on the vertical ruler running down the left of the page. A blue vertical line appears. Drag the line to the 1 metre ruler mark and release the mouse button. A red ruler guide line appears.

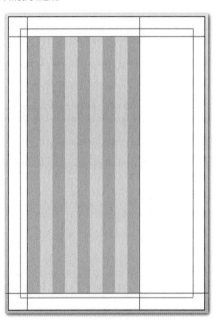

Repeat to place a ruler guide at the 7 metre mark.

4 To create a horizontal rule guide, click on the horizontal ruler running across the top of the page. Drag down to the 1 metre ruler mark and release the mouse button. A red ruler guide line appears.

Repeat to place a guide at the 14 metre mark.

You should now have a 6 m by 13 m area sectioned off with ruler guides.

5 Select your lawn and move it into the area you've just created.

> **To move a ruler guide:**
> Click and drag it—it will follow the current cursor position.
>
> **To remove a ruler guide:**
> Drag and drop it anywhere outside the page area.

With our lawn scaled and in place, we're ready to build the deck!

To create a garden deck

1 On the **Gallery** tab, still in the **Garden/Surfaces and Features** category, locate **Decking section blue** (or **Decking section natural** if you prefer) and drag it over to your page.

The decking sections we intend to purchase come in 1 m x 1 m square sections. Let's scale our decking section to match these dimensions.

Design a Garden

2 Click the ↖ **Pointer** tool and then select the decking section.
Click one of the corner sizing handles and drag it to a new
position while holding down the left mouse button. Release the
mouse button when the decking section measures 1 m
x 1 m (you can also type the dimensions into the **W**
(width) and **H** (height) boxes on the **Transform** tab).

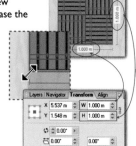

💡 To size your garden elements precisely, it will help if
you zoom in. To do this, click the ⊕ **Zoom In** button—
located on the HintLine toolbar.

We want to build a 6 m by 2 m deck right across the top of our garden. We can do
this by simply cutting and pasting this first section. (You can copy our deck, or create
your own if you prefer a different size or shape.)

3 Right click the decking section and click **Copy**. Right-click again and click **Paste**.

A copy of the object is pasted on top of the original and is automatically selected.

4 Move the two sections into place at the top of the garden (in our example, this
corresponds to the lower edge of the page). Zooming in will help you do this.

5 Select and align the decking sections:

- Draw a selection bounding box around both objects.

- or -

- Select one object, press and hold the **Shift**
  key, and then select the second object.

Now on the **Align** tab, click 🗐 **Align Right**.

6 With the objects still selected, on the Standard
toolbar, click the 🔲 **Group** button. Now right-click
the new group and click **Copy**. Right-click again and
click **Paste**.

7 The copied group is pasted on top of the original
and selected by default. Click and drag it into
place next to the first two sections.

8 Repeat step 5 to align the four sections, this time
clicking 🔟 **Align Bottom**.

9 Repeat the **Copy**, **Paste**, and **Align** procedures to
complete the whole deck.

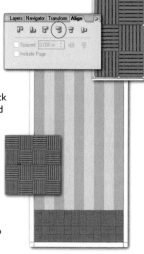

We're pretty excited about the summerhouse, so let's add this next. We also think it would be nice to build a path leading from the deck to the summerhouse, so we'll 'build' that too...

To create a summerhouse and path

1. On the **Gallery** tab, in the **Garden/Buildings and Fixtures** category, locate **Octagon summerhouse** and drag it on to your page.

2. Resize the summerhouse to the dimensions you want to use—ours is 2.5 m wide, and then move it into position in the garden.

If you prefer something simpler, the Gallery also contains a rectangular-shaped summerhouse, called simply '**Summerhouse.**'

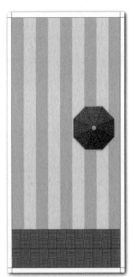

Now for the path. The DrawPlus **Gallery** tab provides a selection of straight and curved path sections to choose from. We think a curved path would look good, but you can choose whichever style you prefer.

3. In the **Garden/Surfaces and Features** category, locate the path section of your choice (we used **Curved path section 1**) and drag it on to your page. Resize the path section by clicking and dragging one of its corner handles. We scaled our path section down to a width of approximately 0.5 m.

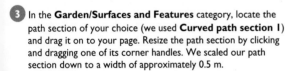

4. Select the path section, right-click, and then click **Copy**. Right-click again and click **Paste**. A copy of the object is pasted on top of the original and is selected by default. Drag this copy off to the side so that you can see both path sections.

5. On the HintLine toolbar, click the ⊕ **Zoom In** button and zoom in on the path sections. Note how they have been designed to allow you to lay them end-to-end.

Now drag the sections into place so that their edges interlock, as illustrated.

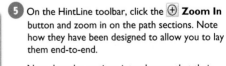

Design a Garden

6 Continue copying and pasting the path sections until your path is long enough to stretch between the deck and the summerhouse.

7 Select the entire path, then on the Standard toolbar, click 🔲 **Group**. Your path sections are combined into a single object, which you can move and resize with ease.

8 Use the ➤ **Pointer** tool to drag the path into position.

- or -

Use the 🔄 **Rotate** tool if you want to place your path at an angle, as we have done.

All we need to do now is change the **order of objects** on the page.

9 Click the summerhouse, then on the Standard toolbar, click the 🔲 **Bring to Front** button. The end of the path disappears behind the summerhouse object.

10 Now click on the decking section that meets the other end of the path. Again, click the 🔲 **Bring to Front** button to bring the deck to the front of the drawing.

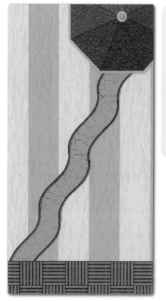

> 💡 **Object order**
>
> Think of the objects on a page as being stacked on top of each other.
>
> Each time you create a new object, it is placed in front of the objects already on the page.
>
> However, you can move any object to any level in the ordering sequence using the **Arrange** menu's **Order Objects** commands.
>
> For more information, see "Ordering objects" in online Help.

Now that you're familiar with the process of adding objects to your garden layout, and scaling and ordering them on your page, you can go ahead and complete your design.

You don't need us to provide step-by-step instructions. We will, however, show you our finished layout and highlight any tips that we think you'll find useful.

Rockery

We dragged the **Rockery corner** symbol from the **Surfaces and Features** category, then added a variety of plants from the **Hedges, Shrubs, and Trees** category.

Borders

We used **Border area 2** from the **Surfaces and Features** category for the main border area, then dragged various trees and shrubs on to it.

For the two areas either side of the path, we used **Bedding area 5**, which we resized and rotated to fit the curve of the path.

Before placing our plants and trees, we clicked the **Bring to Front** button to place the path sections on top of the bedding areas.

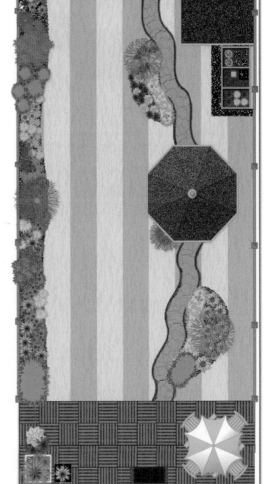

Design a Garden

Patio

We chose **Patio surface 4** to match the colour of the path. If you don't like our choice, you'll find another five patio surfaces in the **Surfaces and Features** category— along with a selection of other surfaces such as bark chip, coir matting, gravel, and pebble (which we used under the cold frame).

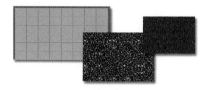

Cold frame

We decided that a cold frame would be adequate for our needs, and for the size of the garden. If you have bigger ideas, however, you can add one of the greenhouses instead. Don't forget to put a few plants inside for authenticity!

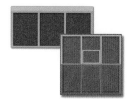

> If you have various design ideas in mind, why not create alternative layouts on different layers. You can then hide and display the layers in different combinations and choose your favourite. You can even use the **Layers** tab to locate (and name) your various garden elements, making it easier to work with them.
>
> For instructions on how to create multi-layered documents, see the online Help, or any one of the following tutorials:
>
> - Make a Clock Face
> - Draw a Gemstone
> - Make a Family Tree
>
> Don't worry—it sounds complicated, but it's really very easy to do!

Potted plants

We livened up our deck and patio with a selection of potted plants. You'll find a range of empty containers 'ready for planting' in the **Containers** category.

Garden furniture

You'll find a selection of garden and patio furniture in the **Buildings and Fixtures** category. Choose a style and a finish—we chose natural wood—and then imagine yourself relaxing in style and enjoying your beautiful new garden!

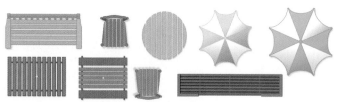

Turn Photos into Art

The DrawPlus **Brushes** tab contains a vast array of pressure-sensitive brush strokes. These powerful tools emulate traditional 'natural media' effects, providing you with a realistic painting or drawing experience. You'll be excited by the possibilities open to you—create pencil sketches, charcoal drawings, watercolours, and oil paintings. You can even experiment with a combination of media effects. The only thing limiting you is your imagination...

In this tutorial, we'll show you how to:

Adjust the pressure sensitivity of your Serif GraphicsPad pen and tablet.

- Build up a composition using layers.

- Apply brush strokes (using either the mouse or a pen and tablet).

- Turn a landscape photograph into a watercolour painting.

- Turn a portrait photograph into a charcoal sketch.

> If you have not yet worked with the Brushes tab and its associated controls, we suggest you complete the Level 1 tutorial, "Use the Natural Media Brushes," before beginning this one.

Turn Photos into Art

Adjusting the pressure sensitivity of the GraphicsPad pen and tablet

We'll start this tutorial by showing you how to customize the **pressure sensitivity** of your Serif GraphicsPad pen and tablet using the **Tablet Properties** dialog. (If you're unfamiliar with the term, pressure sensitivity refers to the amount of pressure needed to click or draw with the pen.)

The **Tablet Properties** dialog contains various other settings that control the behaviour of your pen and tablet. In this section, we'll focus on pressure sensitivity alone; however, we suggest you experiment with all of the settings to discover what works best for you.

This section assumes that you have already installed your Serif GraphicsPad.

For information about installation and setup procedures, refer to the *Serif GraphicsPad User Manual* and tutorials.

Similarly, if you are using a different pen and tablet, refer to the accompanying documentation.

To adjust pressure sensitivity

1 Open the GraphicsPad **Tablet Properties** dialog. You can do this in one of the following ways:

- On the system taskbar, double-click the GraphicsPad icon, or right-click it and choose **Tablet Properties**.

- Double-click the GraphicsPad desktop shortcut that was created when you installed the tablet software.

- Click the Windows **Start** button, choose **All Programs** (for versions other than Windows XP, choose the **Programs** group), choose **Tablet**, then click **Tablet Properties**.

2 In the dialog, drag the slider to achieve a softer or firmer setting. In general:

- Use a firm tip setting when you want maximum control. For example, when drawing thin lines and strokes.

- Use a soft tip setting when you want to create broad strokes, or when a wider range of pressure values is required.

For details on this and other settings, see the *Serif GraphicsPad User Manual*.

When you're happy with your pen and tablet settings, you're ready to open DrawPlus and start painting. Let's begin with a watercolour...

Q The watercolour and portrait files that were created for this tutorial, and the original source images, are provided in your Workspace folder. In a standard installation, you'll find this folder in the following location:

C:\Program Files\Serif\DrawPlus\X2\Tutorials\Workspace

The **Watercolour.dpp** and **Portrait.dpp** files each comprise multiple pages, which you can click through to see how we built up the final image.

We've also included 📑 PageHints to help explain key elements—simply double-click a PageHint icon to open its dialog.

The DrawPlus **Samples** collection also includes the final watercolour and portrait images. To open a sample, in the DrawPlus Startup Wizard, click **View Samples** and then browse to locate the file you want to open.

Example 1: Create a landscape in watercolours

If you love the look of traditional watercolour paintings, you'll be delighted with the DrawPlus watercolour brushes. In this exercise, we'll show you to turn a landscape photograph into a delicate watercolour composition.

1️⃣ In the DrawPlus Startup Wizard, choose **Drawing**, select a Letter or A4 Landscape page size and click **Open**.

2️⃣ On the Drawing toolbar, click the 🖼 **Insert Picture** button, browse to your **Workspace** folder and open the **Landscape.jpg** file.

Resize and position the image so that it takes up most of the page, as illustrated.

3️⃣ Over on the **Layers** tab, you'll see that your document currently contains a single layer—**Layer 1**, containing the photograph.

As we build up our watercolour image, we'll create additional layers for each of the elements of the composition. To begin, let's add a layer for the background—in this case, the sky.

4️⃣ On the **Layers** tab, click the ➕ **Add Layer** button. Right-click the new layer—**Layer 2**— and click **Layer Properties**.

In the **Layer Properties** dialog, in the **Name** box, type a new name for the layer—e.g., 'Sky' or 'Background,' and click **OK**.

Turn Photos into Art

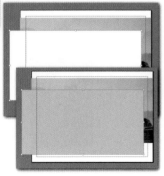

5 On the Drawing toolbar, on the Quick Shapes flyout, click the ☐ **Quick Rectangle** and draw a rectangle the same size as your image. Move the shape down, so that you can see the sky in the original photograph.

6 On the **Swatches** or **Colour** tab, find a colour that matches the sky in the photograph and apply it to the shape.

7 On the **Line** tab, remove the shape's outline by choosing **None** from the style drop-down list.

8 On the Drawing toolbar, click the 🖉 **Paintbrush** tool.

9 On the **Brushes** tab, in the category drop-down list, choose **Watery Paint** and select **Watery Paint 13**.

10 On the Brush context toolbar, change to a wide brush stroke by increasing the **Width** value.

> 💡 When making long sweeping strokes, you'll get the best results if you choose a **repeating brush** (such as Watery Paint 13).
>
> To check if a brush stroke is repeating or non-repeating, right-click it on the **Brushes** tab and select **Edit**.
>
> In the **Body repeat method** box, non-repeating brushes are assigned a **None - Stretch** value; repeating brushes are assigned any other value.

11 On the **Swatches** or **Colour** tab, choose a colour for the sky, and then paint the area using broad sweeping strokes. Don't worry about painting over the edges of the rectangle—we'll tidy up next.

12 On the **Edit** menu, click **Select All**.

On the Standard toolbar, on the 🔲 **Crop/Uncrop** flyout, click **Clip to Bottom**.

The ends of the brush strokes are clipped to the border of the rectangle.

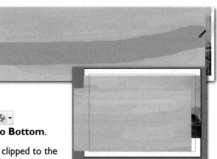

> 💡 As with all brush strokes, the appearance of a watercolour stroke remains adjustable, even after you have moved on to other areas of your painting. You'll find this invaluable as it allows you to experiment with the look of your painting.
>
> To adjust the properties of a brush stroke, use the controls on the **Brush context toolbar**. For details, see online Help or the "Use the Natural Media Brushes" tutorial.

13 Move the shape off the page for now, so that you can see the photograph.

14 On the Drawing toolbar, click the 🖊 **Pen** tool, then click to trace around the outline of the hills in the distance.

- Apply a fill to the shape (you'll need to click the **Fill** button in the top left corner of the **Swatches** or **Colour** tab first).

- Remove its outline.

- Paint over it using broad brush strokes.

15 Use the ↖ **Pointer** tool to draw a selection bounding box around the shape and all the brush strokes.

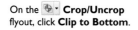

On the 🔲 ▾ **Crop/Uncrop** flyout, click **Clip to Bottom**.

DrawPlus clips the ends of the brush strokes to the border of the shape behind it.

16 Repeat this procedure to trace around all of the objects in the background of the photo.

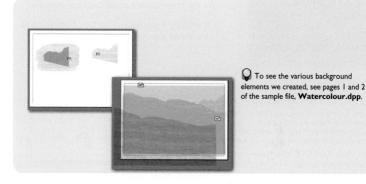

💡 To see the various background elements we created, see pages 1 and 2 of the sample file, **Watercolour.dpp**.

Turn Photos into Art

17 On the **Layers** tab, click the ✚ **Add Layer** button to create a third layer. Name this layer 'Hills.'

On the **Hills** layer, use the technique described previously to create the green hills.

18 Add another layer and rename it 'Grass.' Use this layer to create the bright green grass section in the foreground.

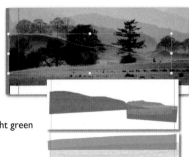

💡 This stage of our composition is shown on page 3 of the **Watercolour.dpp** sample file.

We're now ready to move on to the objects in the foreground of our image.

19 Add another layer and rename it 'Trees.' Use this layer to 'block in' the shapes of the trees and some of the larger foreground areas. Use varying brush widths and strokes to create background shapes on which to add the detail later.

20 Add another layer and rename it 'Tree Detail.' On this layer, use a small brush width to paint in the branches and other details of the trees.

It will help if you zoom into the composition to trace over these detailed areas.

💡 Here, we've hidden the **Sky**, **Hills**, **Grass**, and **Trees** layers so that you can see exactly what we painted on our **Tree Detail** layer. As you are building up your composition, it might help you to focus in on an area if you hide the layers behind the one you are working on. To do this, simply click the 👁 **Hide/Show Layer** button for the layers you want to hide.

21 To complete the watercolour, add two more layers—'Foreground Trees' and 'Foreground Detail.' Again, choose a small brush and zoom into the areas you want to trace.

22 When you are happy with your painting, you can delete **Layer 1**—the layer containing your original image.

To do this, on the **Layers** tab, simply select the layer to delete and then click the 🔲 **Delete** button.

That's it! Your watercolour is complete.

Example 2: Create a portrait in pastels

In this exercise, we'll show you how to turn a portrait photograph into a pastel sketch. Again, you can use our sample file, **Portrait.jpg**, which you'll find in your **Workspace** folder, or you can use one of your own photographs.

For this composition, we used some of the same techniques used in the previous example. In these cases, we have summarized the process rather than repeating it step-by-step.

1 In the DrawPlus Startup Wizard, choose **Drawing**, select a Letter or A4 Portrait page size and click **Open**.

2 On the Drawing toolbar, click the 🖼 **Insert Picture** button, browse to your **Workspace** folder and open the **Portrait.jpg** file (or choose your own image file).

Resize and position the image so that it takes up most of the page.

As we did for our watercolour, we'll create additional layers, slowly building up areas of dark, light, and mid-tones. Finally, we'll add areas of detail such as the eyes and hair. To begin, we'll add a layer for the background.

3 On the **Layers** tab, click the ➕ **Add Layer** button. Name this layer 'Main Background.' Draw a Quick Rectangle the size of the image and apply a rich brown fill to match the background colour.

4 Add another layer and name it 'Backdrop.' On this layer, use a similar brown colour with a medium sized pastel brush (we used 41 pt), to roughly sketch in some texture to the background.

Turn Photos into Art

5 Create another layer and name it 'Skin.' Hide the **Backdrop** layer and, using the original image as reference, choose a smaller width pastel brush (we used 35 pt) to start adding areas of skin tone.

💡 This stage of our composition is illustrated on page 2 of the **Portrait.dpp** sample file.

6 Continue to build up areas of highlights and shadows, creating new layers as you work.

Try to keep all brush strokes fluid and loose.

7 Working with smaller brush strokes, aim to bring out details of the suit, shirt, and tie. However, don't forget that the focus remains on the face.

With final details added—the eyes and wisps of hair—our portrait is complete! (Don't forget to delete the layer containing your original photo!)

In this exercise, we have created two very different styles of painting, using various techniques. Perhaps the most important tip to note is the extensive use of layers in both examples. Using layers like this helps you to slowly build up your image—giving you greater control over the final result.

We hope you've enjoyed this tutorial and are happy with your creations. If you're not, don't be disheartened. As with natural media techniques, painting and sketching with DrawPlus brushes takes time and practice. The more you experiment, the more proficient you will become.

Blend and Animate Objects

Create an animation that morphs between two objects by using the **Blend** tool in conjunction with DrawPlus stopframe animation capabilities.

In this exercise, we'll show you how to:

- Create a new stopframe animation project.

- Create a simple drawing using Quick Shapes.

- Use the **Blend** tool to merge the objects in a series of steps.

- Align and centre objects on a page.

- Distribute blend objects to new animation frames.

- Set frame duration properties.

- Preview an animation and export it to animated GIF and video file formats.

Blend and Animate Objects

1. On the **File** menu, click **New**, then click **New Stopframe Animation**.

2. On the **Tools** menu, click **Options**, click the **Layout** option and then change the **Ruler Units** to pixels. Click **OK**.

3. On the **File** menu, click **Page Setup**. In the **Stopframe Animation Page Setup** dialog, set the dimensions to 200 x 200 pixels and then click **OK**.

4. At the lower edge of the workspace, click the ▬▬▬ **Open/Close** button to display the **Frames** tab. A single blank frame (Frame 1) is displayed in the tab.

5. On the QuickShapes flyout, select the **Quick Clock**. In the upper left corner of the page, click and drag to create a clock face approximately 35 pixels in diameter. Press and hold down the **Ctrl** key while drawing to keep the clock circular.

6. Click the ▶ **Pointer** tool and select the clock. Press and hold the **Ctrl** key and drag a copy down to the lower right corner of your page.

7. With the copied clock selected, on the context toolbar, expand the QuickShapes drop-down list and click **Quick Face**.

8. On the **Swatches** tab, click the ▨ ▾ **Gradient** drop-down list, select a category, and apply a fill to the face. (We've used Linear Fill 42.)

9. Click the ▨ **Blend** tool.

   Click the **Quick Clock** (it will become bounded by a blue box), then click and drag over to the **Quick Face**. Release the mouse button when the **Quick Face** also acquires a blue box.

10. On the Blend context toolbar, set the **Blend Steps** to 10.

11. Click the ▶ **Pointer** tool, then press and hold the **Ctrl** key and click to select the first blend object—the clock.

12. On the **Align** tab, click ▤ **Horizontal Centre** and ▣ **Vertical Centre** to centre the clock on the page.

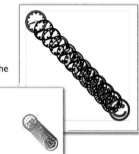

Blend and Animate Objects

13 Repeat steps 11 and 12 to select and centre the last blend object—the face.

The blend objects are now all stacked in the centre of the page.

14 Click the **Blend** tool once again and select the blend objects. On the Blend context toolbar, click 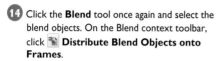 **Distribute Blend Objects onto Frames**.

DrawPlus creates a new frame for each blend object and displays them in the **Frames** tab.

> 🛈 Because we have just one object selected, alignment will be in relation to the page rather than in relation to other objects.

15 On the **Frames** tab, click 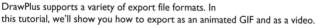 **Properties**.

In the **Animation Properties** dialog, in the **Display each frame for** value box, set the value to 150 milliseconds (ms). Click **OK**.

16 On the **Frames** tab, right click on Frame 1 and click **Properties**.

In the **Frame Properties** dialog, set the display value to 200 ms. Click **OK**.

17 Repeat the previous step to set the display value of **Frame 12** to 200 ms.

18 To preview your animation, click 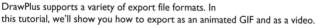 **Preview**.

Now to export the animation.

DrawPlus supports a variety of export file formats. In this tutorial, we'll show you how to export as an animated GIF and as a video.

To export your animation as an animated GIF

1 On the Frames tab, click 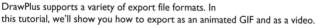 **Export**.

2 In the **Export Optimizer** dialog, accept the default settings and click **Export**.

3 Choose a filename and save location for your file and then click **Save**.

To export your animation as a video

1 On the **File** menu, choose **Export** and then click **Export as Video**.

2 In the **Export to Video** dialog, on the **Basic** tab:

- In the **Filename** box, type a name for your video.

- Click the **Browse** button, browse to locate your save location and click **Save**.

- In the **File** type drop-down list, choose your preferred output file type.

- In the **Template** drop-down list, select an Internet connection speed.

- In the **Quality** drop-down list, select your preferred output file quality.

> Your **Template** and **Quality** choices will depend on the intended audience of your video. For example, if you intend to share your movie on a Web site, think about the connection speed that best suits your audience. The templates are listed in the order of low- to high-speed connections, giving increasing levels of video quality. For more information, see online Help.

3 When you have chosen your export settings, click **Export**.

When the export has completed, the **Export Complete** dialog opens.

4 To view your video file:

- To open the file in the default media player, click **Open**.

- or -

- To open the folder containing the video file, click **Open Folder**. Simply double-click on the file to open it in the default media player.

Create a Movie Viewer

Use keyframe animation to create a movie viewer that you can add to your Web site and use to view a movie clip of your choice.

You'll learn how to:

- Create, edit, and align shapes.

- Use state objects to create **Play** and **Stop** buttons.

- Import movie clips.

- Add action scripts.

- Export your file to Adobe® Flash® file format.

You can use your own movie clip for this project, or our sample, which you'll find in the **Workspace\Animation** folder of your DrawPlus installation directory. In a standard installation, you'll find this folder in the following location:

C:\Program Files\Serif\DrawPlus\X2\Tutorials \Workspace\Animation

Introduction

By default, any object created in DrawPlus is considered to be a **non-state object**, possessing a single set of attributes—colour, transparency, and so on. In keyframe animation, however, you can convert a non-state object to a **state object** by assigning it one or more 'states' (**Normal**, **Hover**, or **Pressed**), each of which possessing its own object attributes.

The key advantage here is that in each state, the object can have a different appearance in response to a user event such as a mouse press or mouse hover over.

In DrawPlus, an object's state is indicated by its adjacent state buttons (only two states will be shown at any time; the third state is the current state).

For example, an object in **Normal** state shows adjacent **Hover** and **Pressed** buttons. If you then click the **Hover** button, you'll jump to that state and the **Normal** and **Pressed** state buttons will display.

In this simple exercise, we'll show you how to create a movie viewer and use state objects to create **Play** and **Stop** buttons that allow you to play and stop a movie clip inside the viewer.

> 💡 You can insert a movie clip into any animation. The movie is inserted into your chosen keyframe as an object, which you can run forward through a specified number of keyframes, or through the entire storyboard, as required.
>
> DrawPlus supports various video formats including .flv, .avi, .mov, .wmv, .mpg, and .swf.

To create the viewer

1. On the **File** menu, point to **New** and then click **New Keyframe Animation**.

2. On the Page context toolbar, in the Page Size drop-down list, click **Large Rectangle**.

3. On the Drawing toolbar, on the QuickShape flyout, click the ☐ **Quick Rectangle**. Draw a large rectangle on your page, leaving space at the bottom of the page for the viewer controls.

4. With the shapes selected:

   - Drag the node up to round the corners.

   - On the **Swatches** tab, click the **Fill** button and then click a mid-grey swatch to apply it to the shape.

5. Right-click the shape and then click **Copy**. Right-click again and click **Paste**.

   DrawPlus pastes a copy of your shape directly on top of the original and selects it by default.

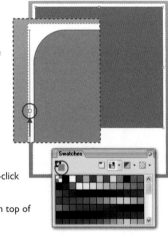

Create a Movie Viewer

⑥ Working with the copied shape, click and drag a corner handle to resize it, and then drag it down to the lower right corner of the large shape.

⑦ Position the small shape so that it extends like a 'tab' beneath the original shape. Click **Edit**, then **Select All** to select both objects, then do the following:

- On the **Align** tab click ▦ **Align Right**.

- On the Standard toolbar, click ▧ **Add**.

    DrawPlus creates a new object that is the composite of both rectangles.

⑧ With the new shape selected, on the Drawing toolbar, click *fx* **Filter Effects**.

- In the **Filter Effects** dialog, select the **Bevel and Emboss** check box and click **OK**.

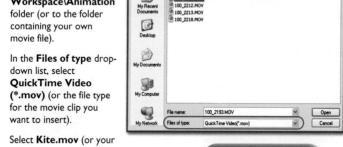

To insert the movie

① On the Drawing toolbar, click ▦ **Insert Movie Clip**.

② In the **Insert Movie Clip** dialog:

- Navigate to your **Workspace\Animation** folder (or to the folder containing your own movie file).

- In the **Files of type** drop-down list, select **QuickTime Video (*.mov)** (or the file type for the movie clip you want to insert).

- Select **Kite.mov** (or your own file) and click **Open**.

③ On your page, position the displayed cursor in the upper left corner of your movie viewer, then click to insert the movie at its original size.

Click and drag out to set the size of the movie inside the viewer, while maintaining its aspect ratio.

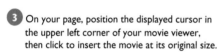

Create a Movie Viewer

4. On the **Layers** tab, locate your movie clip object and then click on its name to highlight it. Rename the clip 'mymovie.'

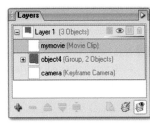

5. On the **Storyboard** tab, in the ▶ ▾ **Preview** drop-down list, select **Preview in Flash Player**.

You should see your movie playing.

To create the state object buttons

1. On the Drawing toolbar, click the ▢ **Quick Rectangle** and draw a small square in the tab area of the viewer.

   - On the **Swatches** tab, set the Line and Fill to red.

2. On the QuickShape flyout, click the ⬠ **Quick Polygon** and draw a small polygon next to the square.

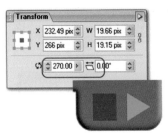

   - On the **Swatches** tab, set the Line and Fill to green.

   - On the context toolbar, set the **Number of sides** to 3 to create a triangle.

   - On the **Transform** tab, set the Rotation to 270°.

3. Move and size the shapes inside the tab area so that they resemble Stop and Play buttons. Select both objects and then on the **Align** tab, click ▥ **Vertical Centre**.

4. Select the red square. On the **Object** menu, choose **State** and then click **Convert to state object**.

5. On the state object toolbar, click the ▦ **Hover** state button. Now let's set the attributes for this button when the user hovers the mouse over it.

6. On the Drawing toolbar, click ƒx **Filter Effects**. In the **Filter Effects** dialog:

   - Select the **Outer Glow** check box.

   - Set the **Blur** to 12 and the **Intensity** to 5.

   - Set the colour to red.

   - Click **OK**.

7 Select the green triangle. Repeat steps 4 to 6, this time setting the outer glow colour to green.

8 Select the red square. On the **Actions** tab, double-click **Mouse Press (Object)**.

9 In the **Mouse Press (Object)** dialog, in the left **Available Actions** pane:

- Expand the **Timeline Actions**, then **Submovies** categories.

- Double-click the **Stop Movie** action (or press the **Add** button).

- In the **Stop submovie Parameters** dialog, select **mymovie** from the drop-down list and click **OK**.

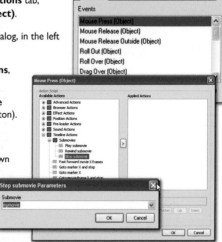

The **Stop Movie** action is added to the **Applied Actions** pane on the right.

- Click **OK** to close the **Mouse Press (Object)** dialog.

10 Select the green triangle. Repeat steps 8 and 9, this time selecting the **Play submovie** action.

Create a Movie Viewer

11 Preview your animation.

Your movie should stop and play when you click the appropriate button. Hovering over the buttons will show the glow effect.

To quickly replace your movie clip:

1. On the **Media** tab, in the drop-down list, choose **Movie Clips**. The lower section of the tab displays your clip.

2. Right click on the clip and choose **Replace Media**. Browse to locate the replacement file and click **Open**.

Create a WebPlus Flash Banner

In this beginner-level project, you'll use basic keyframe animation tools and techniques to create a simple Web banner that you can import into WebPlus 10.

You'll learn how to:

- Create and edit shapes.

- Create and format artistic text.

- Import and resize pictures.

- Select and align objects.

- Create scrolling text and image effects.

- Apply 'fade-in' transparency effects.

- Adjust the rate of change of an animation effect.

- Export to Flash SWF file format.

- Import your banner into WebPlus 10.

- Customize your banner for other projects.

Create a WebPlus Flash Banner

In this exercise, we'll create a WebPlus 10 Flash banner using a preset page size. Of course, if you want to create a different size banner, you can do so.

1 On the **File** menu, point to **New** and then click **New Keyframe Animation**.

2 On the Page context toolbar, set the following page options:

- In the Page Size drop-down list, click **WebPlus 10 Flash Banner**.(or select your own preferred option).

- Click ▢ **Landscape**.

3 On the HintLine toolbar, click ▢ **Fit Page**.

4 On the Drawing toolbar, on the QuickShape flyout, click the ▢ **Quick Rectangle** and draw a large rectangle that almost fills the page.

5 With the rectangle selected, do the following:

- Drag the left sliding node up to round the corners.

- On the **Align** tab, click ▤ **Horizontal Centre** and ▥ **Vertical Centre**.

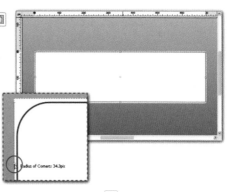

- On the **Swatches** tab, in the ▧ ▾ **Gradient** drop-down list, click **Linear**. Click the red to orange **Linear 180** swatch.

- On the **Line** tab, in the Line Style drop-down list, click **None** to remove the outline.

- On the Drawing toolbar, click *fx* **Filter Effects**. In the **Filter Effects** dialog, select **Bevel and Emboss** and click **OK**.

6 Click on the pasteboard area to deselect your shape, then on the Drawing toolbar, click the **Λ Artistic Text** tool. Click and drag on your page to set the text size and then type some text.

7 Triple-click inside the text object to select all the text and then use the Text context toolbar to apply the font style and size of your choice.

8 Click the ⊾ **Pointer** tool and select the text object. Drag it into the centre left of the shape. On the Drawing toolbar, click ▥ **Insert Picture**.

In the **Insert Picture** dialog, browse to locate a picture for your banner. (You'll need two images in total.) Select the image file you want to add and click **Open**.

On your page:

- Click to insert the picture at default size.

- or -

- Click and drag to set the size of the picture (illustrated).

9 Repeat the previous step to insert a second picture.

10 Resize your pictures as required and position them to the right of your text object.

11 On the **Edit** menu, click **Select All** (or press **Ctrl + A**) and then on the **Align** tab click ▦ **Vertical Centre**.

12 On the **Storyboard** tab, click ▣ **Insert**.

In the **Insert Keyframes** dialog:

- In the **Number of keyframes** box, enter **1**.

- In the **Keyframe duration** box, enter **2.0** seconds.

- Click **OK**.

DrawPlus adds a second keyframe to the **Storyboard** tab.

By default, this keyframe contains all of the objects you created on keyframe 1.

13 Working on the first keyframe, click the ⊾ **Pointer** tool, select the text object and move it to the left so that it sits just outside the page edge.

Create a WebPlus Flash Banner

14 With the first picture selected:

- On the **Transparency** tab, click the **Opacity 0%** swatch to make the picture fully transparent.

15 With the second picture selected:

- Repeat step 14 to make it fully transparent.

- Drag it straight up until it's just above the top page edge.

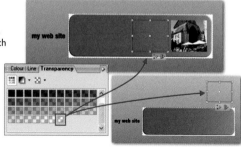

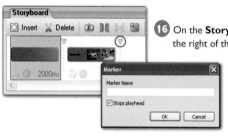

16 On the **Storyboard** tab, click the marker just to the right of the second keyframe.

17 In the **Marker** dialog, select **Stops playhead** and click **OK**.

ℹ️ In the **Marker** dialog, you can also type a name for your marker—it's a good idea to do this when working on more complex project s containing multiple markers.

18 On the **File** menu, click **Preview in Flash Player**.

Your Web banner animation will now play once and then stop, rather than looping continuously.

Our Web banner looks great, but let's make one final adjustment to improve the effect.

Currently, our animation runs at a constant speed from start to finish, which is the default behaviour. However, DrawPlus allows us to adjust the rate of change of various aspects of an animation—position, transparency, colour, and so on—using **envelopes**.

To demonstrate this, we'll adjust all the envelopes in our animation to produce an 'acceleration' effect.

19 Open keyframe 1 in the workspace and click **Ctrl + A** to select everything on the page.

On the **Easing** tab, in the drop-down list, select **All Envelopes**. In the profile pane, click and drag on the blue line to create a gentle curve. (You may need to expand the **Easing** tab to use the profile pane.)

20 Preview your animation again to see the result of your envelope adjustments.

If required, you can continue adjusting the envelope profile until you achieve a result you are happy with.

Now to export your Web banner.

21 On the **File** menu, choose **Export** and then click **Export as Flash SWF**.

Choose a file name and save location for your .swf file and then click **Save**.

The **Keyframe Animation Export** dialog displays the progress of the export and closes when export is complete. .

Simply browse to locate the file and then double-click to open it.

To import your Web banner into WebPlus 10

1 Open WebPlus 10.

2 Open an existing site or create a new one from scratch.

3 Open the **Master A** page in the workspace. On the Web Objects toolbar, on the Media flyout, click **Insert Flash file**.

💡 **Master pages**
We recommend that you insert your banner on a master page.

You can then use the **Master Page Manager** to select on which pages you want your banner to appear (default is **All Pages**).

Create a WebPlus Flash Banner

4 In the **Flash** dialog:

- Click the **Browse** button and browse to locate your .swf file.

- Select any other required options—for example, we selected the **Transparent Background** option along with the default settings.

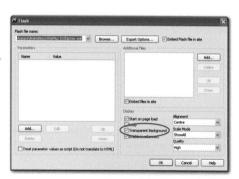

- Click **OK**.

5 Click on your page to insert your Flash banner.

Resize and position as required.

Congratulations, you've created your first Web banner!

But before moving on to the next exercise, let's take a look at how you can use it as a template and quickly adapt it to fit with other Web site projects.

To customize your Web banner

1 Open your Web banner project file in DrawPlus and open the **Media** tab.

The **Media** tab provides a quick and easy to way to view, access, edit, and replace all the bitmap images, movie clips, audio clips, and text fragments in your project.

2 In the drop-down list, select **Bitmap Images**.

The two pictures used in your project are displayed. Right-click an image and click **Replace Media**. Browse to locate a different image and click **Open**.

DrawPlus replaces all instances of the original image with the new selection.

3 In the drop-down list, select **Text Fragments**. The text fragment you created displays in the tab—double-click it.

In the **Replace Text Fragment** dialog. the upper **Replace:** section displays the original text. Type your replacement text in the lower **With:** section and click **OK** to apply it.

Create a Cartoon Animation

DrawPlus X2 provides exciting new functionality that lets you create and export Adobe® Flash®-based animations using keyframes. Combine this with the extensive drawing capabilities of DrawPlus, and you have all the tools you need to create impressive movies, cartoons, Web banners, and so on.

This exercise introduces you to the basic concepts and essential tools, and shows you how to create a simple animated cartoon. You'll learn how to:

- Create a cartoon character using the DrawPlus drawing tools.

- Work with layers and grouping.

- Use keyframes to animate a character.

- Use the AutoRun feature to automatically update object creation and placement as you work.

- Use an object envelope to modify an object's rate of change over time.

- Add a background.

- Export to Adobe® Shockwave Flash® format.

Create a Cartoon Animation

You can view the sample DrawPlus file we created for this project (**Dog_animation.dpa**) and the output file (**Dog_animation.swf**) in the **Workspace\Animation** folder of your DrawPlus installation.

In a default installation, you'll find this folder in the following location:

C:\Program Files\Serif\DrawPlus\X2\Tutorials\Workspace\Animation

You can also use DrawPlus to produce stopframe animations. For an example, see the "Create a Stopframe Animated Cartoon" tutorial.

Introduction

The term **stopframe** (or **stop motion**) animation describes the conventional animation technique that makes static objects appear to move. The object is moved by very small amounts in successive frames, giving the impression of movement when the film is played.

In **keyframe** animation, a particular event or sequence of events is recreated in a series of snapshot images. The event is 'captured' at key moments (keyframes) where an object begins or ends an action. Animation between these keyframes is then calculated by the software—in this case, DrawPlus.

For example, suppose you want to create an animation of a bouncing ball. As the animator, you specify the start, end, and key intermediary positions of the ball, then DrawPlus smoothly fills in the gaps (a process known as **tweening**). At any point, you can fine-tune the animation to improve the duration, speed, and dynamics of the movement by adding or adjusting keyframes.

In the following sections, we'll use the same technique to animate a simple character. Before we can get started on the animation phase of our project, however, there are a few things we need to do.

1: Storyboarding

A storyboard is a visual script of the shots and scene changes in a video or film—a plan that you can refer to as you work on your project.

The storyboarding process helps you to think about how you want your finished animation to look, how the story should unfold, and how best to convey your story to your audience.

Think about what you actually want to achieve, and then create a rough illustration of what will happen during the animation. You don't have to be an artist—rough sketches and stick figures will do just as well.

The storyboard on the left illustrates the animation we are about to create.

2: Starting the project and drawing the character

To begin, let's open DrawPlus, start a new animation project and then draw our character.

To start a new keyframe animation

1. On the **File** menu, point to **New**, then click **New Keyframe Animation**.

DrawPlus creates the first keyframe for the project and displays it in the main work area and on the **Storyboard** tab at the lower edge of the workspace.

(If you can't see the **Storyboard** tab, click the **Open/Close** ▬▬ button at the bottom of the workspace.)

2. On the context toolbar, click ▭ **Landscape** page orientation. Now to create our character.

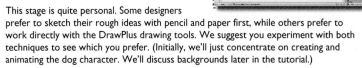

This stage is quite personal. Some designers prefer to sketch their rough ideas with pencil and paper first, while others prefer to work directly with the DrawPlus drawing tools. We suggest you experiment with both techniques to see which you prefer. (Initially, we'll just concentrate on creating and animating the dog character. We'll discuss backgrounds later in the tutorial.)

- If you're sketching with DrawPlus tools, we recommend you use **QuickShapes** for drawing simple shapes, the ✏ **Pencil** tool for drawing freeform lines and shapes, and the ✎ **Pen** tool for precise lines.

> 💡 For step-by-step instructions on creating this simple 'Catboy' character using **QuickShapes** and the **Pencil** tool, see the "Design a Cartoon Movie Poster" Drawing Project.

- You can fine-tune any line or curve by switching to the ▷ **Node** tool and then adjusting the nodes and curves.

- If you have a drawing on paper that you'd like to use as the basis for your animation, scan it into your computer, save it as a graphics file, and then clean it up in DrawPlus (see next section). For information about importing scanned images, see online Help.

- If you're using a pen and tablet but are not too sure of your freehand drawing ability, you can place a printed image on the tablet and trace around its outlines, or draw accurate lines by using a ruler on the tablet.

- If you want to use the character used in this project, you'll find the sample file (**Dog_original.png**) in your **Workspace\Animation** folder.

Create a Cartoon Animation

3: Cleaning up your sketch

When you have created your rough sketch, the next task is to clean up the outlines and shapes. During this stage, you also want to identify and isolate the components that will be moving independently—if you do this, you'll find it easier to adjust and manipulate these parts as you work on your animation keyframes later.

These components will vary depending on your character and story, and will range from the obvious—for example, body, legs, head—to the not so obvious (eyebrows, ears, hair, lips, and so on). Don't go into too much detail at first though. Often, the simpler characters are the most effective, and you can always add more detail later if necessary.

The following tips will help you to achieve the best results:

- If you're working from a scanned image, place your original sketch on Layer 1, add a new layer and then work on this layer as you carefully trace over the original lines.

  When you've finished, hide the layer containing the original sketch to check your results.

- Use **QuickShapes** for simple shapes.

  If necessary, use the ⬡ **Convert to Curves** command and then use the ▷ **Node** tool to adjust the shape. You can do this by clicking and dragging the nodes, curve segments, and control handles. The following illustration shows how we created the basic ear shape from a simple **Quick Ellipse**.

- When using the **Pencil** tool, increase the **Smoothness** on the context toolbar. This reduces the number of nodes on the line, resulting in a 'cleaner,' smoother effect. (We set **Smoothness** to 100%.)

 Optimizing file size

- To keep your Flash files as small as possible, you should avoid using special effects such as filter effects, shadows, 3D, transparency, bitmap fills, and so on, which are also output as bitmaps.

- You can achieve some great simple 'hand-drawn effect' animations with the ✏ **Paintbrush** tool. However, you should try to avoid using the **Paintbrush** if you intend exporting your project to Flash format. This is because brushstrokes are output as bitmaps and will result in a large file size.

Create a Cartoon Animation

- **Group** your items.

  When you've finished drawing the various lines and shapes that make up each component, select them all, then click the **Group** button below the selection.

  You'll now be able to move and rotate all the objects in the group at the same time. You'll find this useful when you are animating the project.

  (To select and edit individual objects within groups, hold down the **Ctrl** key and then click to select.)

- If you need to rotate a component or group of components that are 'hinged' from a fixed point—a leg, arm, or head for example—you'll achieve a more realistic effect if you move the centre of rotation to the hinge point.

  To do this, select the object or group , click the **Rotate** tool, and then click and drag the centre marker to the desired position.

  The illustration below shows how we could use this technique to rotate the head of our cartoon dog.

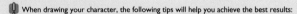

When drawing your character, the following tips will help you achieve the best results:

- Keep it simple and use clean lines and shapes. You can create a detailed version first, to get a good feel for your character, but before you start animating it, you'll need to simplify it. The simpler your character is, the easier it will be to animate.

- Keep your colours simple and in blocks rather than random lines. This will make it easier for you to blend the moving elements of your drawing, and will also help minimize your final file size.

- Use shadows to 'ground' and add depth to your animation. Without shadows, your characters will appear to float.

- If your character is going to talk, you'll need to draw variations of the mouth for different 'sounds.' If you don't require too much detail, you can get by with a few basic mouth shapes—A, E, I, O, U, F, M, P, S, TH, and so on. You'll also need some transition shapes to take you from one mouth form to the next.

- You may need to move small body parts individually at times, but you'll save yourself a lot of effort by creating groups of parts that you can move and rotate together.

Create a Cartoon Animation

The illustration on the right shows our initial sketch and the finished character after tracing and redrawing.

Notice how the addition of the shadow grounds the character and adds depth to the animation.

4: Animating the character

When you are happy with your character, you're ready to animate it.

1 On the **Storyboard** tab, click ▣ **Insert**.

2 In the **Insert Keyframes** dialog:

- In the **Number of keyframes** box, enter **6**.

- In the **Keyframe duration** box, enter **0.333**.

- Click **OK**.

You'll now see seven keyframes on the **Storyboard** tab.

Let's refer to our storyboard to see which parts of the dog we need to adjust. In our example, the head and face have not changed, only the legs have moved.

3 In **keyframe 1**, select all of the objects that make up the dog and his shadow. Click **Edit** and then click **Copy** (or click **Ctrl + C**).

4 Click **keyframe 2** to open in the work area. On the **Layers** tab, click ✛ **Add Layer**.

- Make **Layer 2** the active layer by clicking it on the **Layers** tab to highlight it. Click **Edit** and then click **Paste** (or click **Ctrl + V**) to copy the dog and shadow onto this layer.

- Now make **Layer 1** the active layer and paste another copy of the dog and shadow onto this layer. Delete the body and legs.

  To check that you've done this correctly, hide Layer 2 by clicking its 👁 **Hide/Show** button—you will only see the dog's head and shadow.

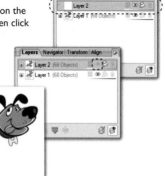

Create a Cartoon Animation

5 On Layer 1, draw the 'new' body and legs shape. Use the body shape on Layer 2 as a reference to ensure that the parts of the body that do not move (the upper chest and back for example), remain in the same position on the page.

Check your progress by periodically hiding the original drawing on Layer 2.

When you have completed your drawing on Layer 1, you can delete Layer 2 by selecting it on the **Layers** tab and then clicking 🔲 **Delete Layer**.

6 Copy and paste the dog and shadow from keyframe 1 onto keyframe 3.

7 Copy and paste the dog and shadow from keyframe 2 onto keyframe 4.

8 Copy and paste the dog and shadow from keyframe 1 onto keyframe 5.

9 Copy and paste the dog and shadow from keyframe 2 onto keyframe 6.

10 Copy and paste the dog and shadow from keyframe 1 onto keyframe 7.

You're storyboard should now resemble ours.

11 Open keyframe 6 in the work area. In this scene, the dog is hit by the bone.

You can keep the basic head shape, but need to redraw the eyes and ears and add the 'bash' star shape.

When you've completed all the changes you need to make to the dog, you can add the bone...

Create a Cartoon Animation

12 On the **Storyboard** tab, click the 🖼 **AutoRun** button to enable this feature.

By default, any new objects you create (and reposition) on any keyframe will now automatically run to the end of the storyboard.

13 Open keyframe 2 in the work area and draw and colour the bone.

Place it in the upper left corner so that only the end is visible.

If you now take a look at your storyboard, you'll see that DrawPlus has placed a copy of the bone in all subsequent keyframes.

14 Open keyframe 3. Click on the bone to select it, and then drag it slightly down and to the right.

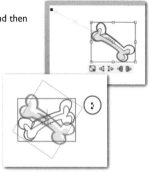

Hover your cursor just outside one of the corner handles. When the cursor changes to the Rotate cursor, click and drag to rotate the bone.

Because you have **AutoRun** enabled, DrawPlus updates the placement of the bone in subsequent keyframes, allowing you to easily make incremental changes to its position.

15 Repeat step 14 to move and rotate the bone through the remaining frames. Remember that it should hit the dog's head in keyframe 6, and then bounce off in keyframe 7.

Notice the path and nodes showing the movement of the bone through the scene.

16 To preview your animation, on the **Storyboard** tab, in the ▶ **Preview** drop-down list, click **Preview in Flash Player**.

17 If required, make any adjustments to the placement of the bone. Preview your animation until you are happy with the results and then click the 🖼 **AutoRun** button to turn this feature off again.

When you preview your animation, you'll see that the dog and bone both move at a constant speed throughout the entire animation. This may be the effect you require, but suppose you want to vary the speed of an object as it moves through a scene. In the next section, we'll show you how to do this.

5: Adjusting object envelopes

When you select an object that is part of a 'run sequence' (such as the bone in our animation), the **Easing** tab becomes available.

In DrawPlus keyframe animations, the **Easing** tab provides a drop-down list of **envelopes** (Position, Morph, Scale, Rotation, Skew, Colour, and Transparency).

All of these envelopes work in similar ways to control how an object's properties change over time, from keyframe to keyframe. Once you learn how to display and modify one type of envelope, you can apply the same principle to the others.

By default, DrawPlus applies a constant rate of change to all envelopes, but you can adjust this by modifying the envelope profile settings.

In this section, we'll make the bone object appear to accelerate as it bounces off the dog's head by applying and modifying a **position envelope**.

The lower section of the **Easing** tab provides various other options that you can apply to the selected object or to the whole run.

To apply a position envelope

1 Open keyframe 6 and select the bone object.

2 On the **Easing** tab, expand the Envelopes drop-down list and select the **Position Envelope**.

Below the drop-down list, in the Envelope Profile pane, the blue diagonal line represents the rate of change of the bone's position from this keyframe to the next.

By default, the rate of change is constant, but we can change this by adjusting the gradient of the profile.

3 Click a point in the middle of the blue line and drag it up to the top of the pane. (You may need to undock and then expand the **Easing** tab to adjust the profile.)

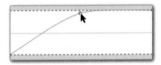

4 Preview your animation again.

You should see the bone speed up as it bounces of the dog's head.

Create a Cartoon Animation

6: Adding a background

You may not need or want a background for your animation. It all depends on your subject matter and the final effect you want to achieve.

A background will provide 'context' for your character, but can also be useful for adding perspective and depth to a scene. There are several ways to do this, for example:

- Use strong (saturated) colours for your character and foreground, and less strong (unsaturated) colours for background objects. (See our circular background below.)

- Make foreground elements sharp and clear and your background elements blurred.

Backgrounds don't have to be detailed. In this racehorse storyboard, the roughly-sketched background gives the impression of motion and speed.

In some cases, a background will reduce the impact of the scene.

Suppose you are animating a stick figure such as the one pictured on the right. Here, you want the viewer's attention to be focused on the character and nothing else.

If you do use a background, place it on a separate layer, underneath all of your other layers.

We created a colourful circular background, which rotated throughout the run sequence.

To add and rotate a circular background

1 Create your background as a DrawPlus .dpp file and export it to .png file format.

2 In your animation, add a new layer and move it down to the bottom of the layers list.

3 On the background layer, click 🖼 **Insert Picture** and position your background graphic.

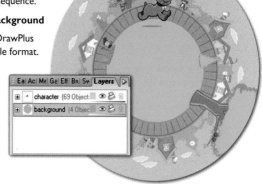

4 Run the image forward to the end of the storyboard by clicking  **Run Forward**.

5 Open the last keyframe, select the background graphic, and then rotate it into its final position. DrawPlus will calculate the steps in between for you.

As it stands, this is a short seven-frame animation, so you don't need to make the rotation angle too big. (If you do want to rotate through the full 360°, you'll need to insert more keyframes—we needed 17 for our example—so that the speed of the rotation is appropriate for the speed of the running dog.)

6 Preview your animation and make any adjustments to the rotation angle if required.

If you're looking for something simpler, you could add a linear background scene.

To add a linear background

1 Repeat steps 1 to 4 of the previous procedure.

2 In the last keyframe, select the background graphic and drag it to the left and into its final position.

3 Preview your animation and make any adjustments if required.

If you're happy with your animation, you're ready to export it.

7: Exporting your animation

You can export to the following formats:

- Adobe Shockwave Flash file (.swf)

- Video (choose from .mov, .stv, .avi, .wmf file formats)

- Screensaver (.scr)

- Flash Lite/ i-Mode (a lightweight version of .swf, optimized for viewing on mobile phones and other devices)

As well as showing changes in position and rotation, you can use keyframes to show changes in colour.

Simply set the start and end colours in separate keyframes and DrawPlus will use tweening to calculate the blend from one colour to the next. You may also want to add an extra keyframe or two for transition stages, as we've done in this example.

To change the rate at which an object's colour changes over time, adjust its **colour envelope**. For example, you could make the blush on this character's face appear quickly and fade away slowly.

Create a Cartoon Animation

For this project, we will export our animation to a standard Shockwave Flash .swf file.

To export to Adobe Shockwave Flash

1 On the **File** menu, point to **Export** and then click **Export as Flash SWF**.

2 Choose a file name and save location for your .swf file and then click **Save**.

3 The **Keyframe Animation Export** dialog displays the progress of the export and closes when export is complete. .

Simply browse to locate the file and then double-click to open it.

We hope that you have enjoyed working through this project and are happy with the resulting animation. We hope that you are now comfortable with the basics of keyframe animation and are ready to begin experimenting with your own projects.

If you'd like to work through some more step-by-step examples, take a look at the other tutorials in the **Animation Projects** section.

Create an Animated Web Banner

You don't have to be an experienced DrawPlus user to create impressive animation effects.

In this project, we'll show you how to use masks and transparency effects to create professional-looking results. We'll create a Web banner, but you can apply the same techniques to any animation project.

- Draw lines and shapes.

- Apply and customize a gradient fill.

- Create and format text.

- Add transparency effects.

- Use a mask to gradually reveal an object on the page.

- Fit text to a curve.

- Work with layers and grouping.

- Preview and export to Adobe® Flash® format.

Create an Animated Web Banner

Introduction

We created our Web banner on five layers. To make it easier to follow, this tutorial is divided into sections, each of which will explain how to create a different layer.

> 🔍 You can view the sample file we created for this project (**Arts_&_Crafts_animation.dpa**) in the **Workspace\Animation** folder of your DrawPlus installation.
>
> In a default installation, you'll find this folder in the following location:
>
> **C:\Program Files\Serif\DrawPlus\X2\Tutorials\Workspace\Animation**

Layer 1: Background

On this layer, we'll create the background elements of our design—the gradient filled rectangle with its brush stroke effect outline, and the large green letter R.

1 On the **File** menu, point to **New** and then click **New Keyframe Animation**.

2 On the Page context toolbar, set the following page options:

- In the Page Size drop-down list, click **Full Banner**.
- Click the 🔲 **Landscape** button.

3 On the Drawing toolbar, on the QuickShape flyout, click the 🔲 **Quick Rectangle** and draw a large rectangle that fills the page.

4 With the rectangle selected, click the **Swatches** tab. In the 🔲 ▾ **Gradient** drop-down list, click **Radial**, and then click the **Radial 1** swatch.

5 On the Drawing toolbar, click the 🔷 **Fill** tool to display the fill path and nodes.

Drag the right node to the left and into position just below the page border. Drag the left node to the right. (See illustration on the right.)

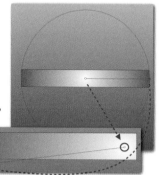

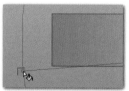

6 On the **Swatches** tab, click the ▷ **Swatches Tab Menu** and select **List View**. In the 🔲 ▾ **Palettes** drop-down list, click **Standard RGB**. Scroll down the palette to locate the **RGB (156, 156, 0)** swatch and then click and drag it over to the leftmost node of your fill path.

Create an Animated Web Banner

Now find the **RGB (252, 252, 156)** swatch and click and drag it over to the rightmost node of your fill path.

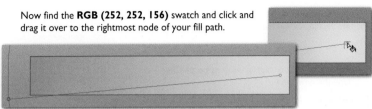

7 On the Drawing toolbar, click the **A** **Artistic Text** tool.

Click and drag on your page to create a large text insertion point, then type the first letter of your banner logo in uppercase.

8 Triple-click the text to select it, then format as follows:

- On the Text context toolbar, change the font to **Ancestory SF**.

- On the **Swatches** tab, apply the **RGB (156, 156, 0)** swatch.

- If required, resize the text by clicking and dragging a corner handle.

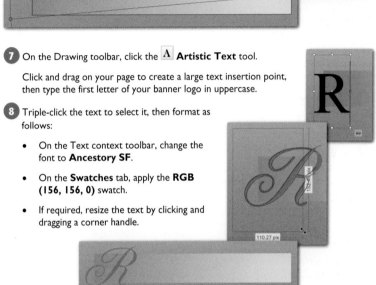

9 Click the **▢** **Quick Rectangle** and draw another rectangle the same size as your first shape.

10 With the new rectangle selected:

- On the **Swatches** tab, remove the fill by clicking the grey and white ■ **None** swatch.

- On the **Swatches** tab, click the **Line** swatch and then click the **RGB (132, 132, 0)** swatch.

- On the **Brushes** tab, click the **Pastel 15 brush** stroke to apply it to the outline.

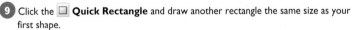

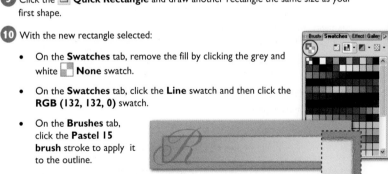

Create an Animated Web Banner

Over on the **Layers** tab, under **Layer I**, you should now see
the two rectangles and the single text object listed.

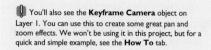

11 On the **Layers** tab, rename your layer 'Background.'

To do this, click to highlight the name and then
type the new name.

Let's move on and create our next layer.

Layer 2: Swish

On our second layer, we'll add the
ornate curved 'swish' design.

1 On the **Layers** tab, click ✥
Add Layer.

Rename the new layer 'Swish.'

> 💡 You'll also see the **Keyframe Camera** object on
> Layer I. You can use this to create some great pan and
> zoom effects. We won't be using it in this project, but for a
> quick and simple example, see the **How To** tab.

2 On the Drawing toolbar, click
the 🖋 **Pen** tool and then click
to create a large closed curved shape across your page. Fill the shape with **RGB (156,
156, 0)**.

Don't worry about drawing a perfect shape—you can edit it in the next step.

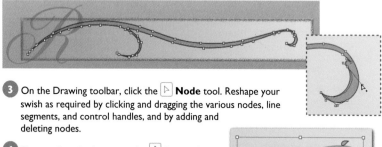

3 On the Drawing toolbar, click the ▷ **Node** tool. Reshape your
swish as required by clicking and dragging the various nodes, line
segments, and control handles, and by adding and
deleting nodes.

4 To complete this layer, use the 🖋 **Pen** tool to
create some leaf shapes, and add a white ○
Quick Ellipse.

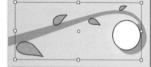

> 💡 The **Pen** tool is a powerful tool that you can use in several different ways. Once you've drawn your
> curve or shape, you can fine-tune it with the **Node** tool—again, using several different methods.
>
> For details, see the **How To** tab or online Help. For a step-by-step exercise, see the Level I tutorial,
> "Work With Line Tools."

Layer 3: Mask

We'll create our mask on layer three, using it to gradually display the elements we've created on our **Swish** layer.

1. On the **Layers** tab, click ✦ **Add Layer**. Rename the new layer 'Mask.'

2. Working on the **Mask** layer, click the ▢ **Quick Rectangle** and draw a long, narrow rectangle to cover the start of the swish.

   This rectangle shape will act as a 'window' through which the swish will appear.

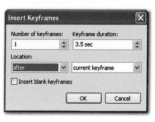

3. With the mask shape selected, on the **Swatches** tab, apply a bright colour to the fill and outline.

   It doesn't matter what colour you choose for your mask as it won't be seen in the final animation. However, when working with masks, it's generally a good idea to make them bright and easily identifiable (especially when working on complex projects).

4. At the bottom of the workspace, on the **Storyboard** tab, click ▣ **Insert**.

   In the **Insert Keyframes** dialog, choose to insert 1 keyframe with a duration of 3.5 seconds and click **OK**.

   On the **Storyboard** tab, DrawPlus adds a new keyframe containing all of your design elements, and displays the project length as 3500 milliseconds (3.5 seconds).

5. On the **Storyboard** tab, click ▥ **Split**. In the **Split Keyframe** dialog, type '6' and click **OK**.

   All your design elements, including the mask, now run right through to the end of the animation.

6. On the **Storyboard** tab, click on the last keyframe to open it in the workspace. On the **Layers** tab, click on the **Mask** layer.

7. Select the mask object, then click and drag the right sizing handle until the shape completely covers the swish.

Create an Animated Web Banner

8 On the **Layers** tab, right-click the **Mask** layer
and click **Layer Properties**. In the **Layer
Properties** dialog, in the **Attributes** section:

- Select the **Locked** check box.

- Select the **Mask** check box and then in the
  drop-down layers list, select **1**.

- This tells DrawPlus that we want this layer
  to only mask one layer beneath it. (If we'd
  chosen to mask 2 layers, the mask would
  also hide objects on the **Background** layer.)

- Click **OK**.

On the **Layers** tab, the  **Mask** and
Locked icons now display next to the **Mask** layer.

9 On the **Storyboard** tab, in the **Preview** list, click
Preview in Flash Player.

10 If necessary, in the first and last keyframes, adjust the start and end position and size of
the mask until you're happy with the way in which it reveals the swish.

Now we'll add two more layers **above** our mask layer.

Layer 4: Logo

On our next layer, we'll add our logo and some flower shapes. We don't want these
elements to appear immediately, so we'll stagger their appearance on the storyboard.

1 On the **Layers** tab:

- Click **Add Layer**. Rename the new layer 'Logo & Flowers.'

- Click the **Hide/Show** layer button next to your **Mask** layer. This hides the
  mask so that you can see the entire swish on all your keyframes. (You don't have
  to do this but it helps to see the whole design while you are adding new elements
  to it.)

2 Open keyframe 4 in the workspace.

- Click the **Λ** **Artistic Text** tool and create a logo in the left section of the
  banner, on top of your background letter.

- Resize the logo text to about 32 pts.

- Apply the Ancestry SF font.

- On the **Swatches** tab, in the
  Gradient drop-down list, click **Linear** and
  then apply the **Linear 119** swatch.

Create an Animated Web Banner

 Click the  **Pen** tool.

Use your preferred drawing method to create a flower head out of a series of closed and filled curves.

4 Select all the elements that make up your flower head and then click the **Group** button.

5 With the flower selected, on the **Transparency** tab, apply the **Opacity 70%** swatch.

6 Copy and paste the flower head and apply the **Opacity 22%** swatch.

7 Position the two flower heads in the middle section of the banner.

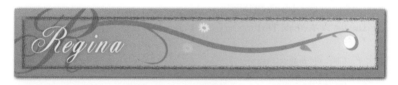

8 On the **Edit** menu, click **Select All** to select the logo and both flowers.

- To the lower right of the selection, click **Run Forward**. In the **Run Forward** dialog, select **To end of storyboard** and click **OK**.

- On the **Storyboard** tab, if you now click through the keyframes, you'll see that DrawPlus has run these three objects right through to the last keyframe.

9 Right-click one of the flower heads and click **Copy**.

- Open keyframe 3 in the workplace, then right-click on the page and click **Paste** to add a copy of the flower to this keyframe.

- Increase the size of the copied flower.

- Apply the **Opacity 78%** swatch from the **Transparency** tab.

- Position the flower as illustrated, right.

- Select the flower, then click **Run Forward**. In the **Run Forward** dialog, select **To end of storyboard** and click **OK**.

Create an Animated Web Banner

10 Open keyframe 5 and add another copy of the flower.

- Position the flower towards the end of the swish shape.

- Select the flower, then click ▶▶ **Run Forward**.

- In the **Run Forward** dialog, select **To end of storyboard** and click **OK**.

11 Preview your animation and make any adjustments, as required.

Just one more layer to create...

5: Text on a curve

On our final layer, we'll create a text object and fit it to the curve of the swish.

1 On the **Layers** tab, click ➕ **Add Layer**. Rename the new layer 'Curve Text.'

2 Open keyframe 5 in the workspace.

Use the **A Artistic Text** tool to create a text object containing the words 'Arts & Crafts.'

- Click and drag to resize the text to about 15 pts (or use the context toolbar.)

- On the context toolbar, apply the Gelfing SF font.

- On the **Swatches** tab, apply the **RGB (88, 84, 0)** swatch to the text fill.

- Position the text object just inside the 'dip' of the swish.

3 Select the text object then on the Text context toolbar, click to expand the ✎ **Curved Text** flyout.

- Click the **Bottom Circle** preset curve.

DrawPlus fits your text into a 'U' curve.

4 On the Drawing toolbar, click the ▷ **Node** tool.

Edit the curve text to fit along the swish by dragging the nodes and curve handles.

5 With the text object selected:

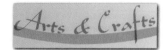

- On the **Transparency** tab, apply the **Opacity 50%** swatch.

- Click ▶▶ **Run Forward** and run the text through to the end of the storyboard.

6 Open keyframe 6 and select the curve text object:

- On the **Transparency** tab, apply the **Opacity 100%** swatch.

- On the object toolbar, click ⬐▷ **Update attributes forward**.

- In the **Update Forward** dialog, select **To end of storyboard**. Click **OK**.

This tells DrawPlus to apply 100% opacity to the remainder of the 'run' of the curve text object. (In this example, there is only one more keyframe in the run.)

7 Preview your animation and make any final adjustments, as required.

When you're happy with your animated banner, you're ready to export it.

⬐▷ **Update attributes forward**

⬐▷ **Update attributes backward**

Click to apply a selected object's attributes (fill, line, effects, etc.) to the same object in subsequent or previous keyframes, or to the start or end of the storyboard.

Create an Animated Web Banner

Export to Adobe Shockwave Flash

For this project, we will export our animation to a standard Adobe® Shockwave Flash® .swf file.

To export as Flash

1 On the **File** menu, point to **Export** and then click **Export as Flash SWF**.

2 Choose a file name and save location for your .swf file and then click **Save**.

3 The **Keyframe Animation Export** dialog displays the progress of the export and closes when export is complete.

Simply browse to locate the file and then double-click to open it.

Congratulations, you've reached the end of the project! We hope that you have enjoyed learning how to use masks in DrawPlus animations. With a little bit of practise, we're sure you'll soon be using them to create impressive, dynamic effects.

If you'd like to work through some more step-by-step animation examples, take a look at the other tutorials in the **Animation Projects** section.

Add Animation to a Web Site

Add interactivity to your animation projects by assigning events (for example, mouse click, hover over) and associated actions (display/hide an object, move an object, etc) to the objects on your page.

Don't worry, you don't have to be an experienced programmer. DrawPlus includes a whole range of preset actions that you can assign to your objects with just a few mouse clicks.

In this project, we'll create an interactive Web page for a T-shirt company. You'll learn how to:

- Create and edit shapes.

- Apply transparency and gradient fill effects.

- Use the Replicate command to create a grid of objects.

- Use masks to hide and display objects.

- Create Hover state objects.

- Use actions to move objects, change object colour, and switch pages when a button is pressed.

- Export to Adobe® Shockwave Flash®.

> 💡 Aimed at more advanced users, this project assumes that you have some experience with basic DrawPlus tools and techniques.
>
> In addition, if you have not worked with events and actions, we suggest you work through the "Create a Movie Viewer" animation project before starting this one.

Add Animation to a Web Site

> You'll find our DrawPlus project file (**T-shirts.dpa**), and the exported output file (**T-shirts.swf**), in the **Workspace\Animation** folder of your DrawPlus installation directory. In a default installation, you'll find this at the following location:
>
> **C:\Program Files\Serif\DrawPlus\X2\Tutorials\Workspace\Animation**

Introduction

In this project, we'll create a Web page that allows users to select from a range of T-shirt styles, then add a design and choose a colour for the design. When our layout is complete, we'll use the **Actions** tab to specify events and actions for each button.

DrawPlus makes use of **ActionScript**, a language specifically designed for Adobe® Flash® applications, to allow a high level of interactivity between the exported Flash SWF file and the user (in this case a Web visitor). DrawPlus supplies a wide range of preset actions, but you can also add your own custom scripts. In this project, we'll be using preset actions.

This project is broken down into the following sections:

1. Setting up the project and basic layout.

2. Creating the t-shirt styles and mask.

3. Creating the design styles and mask.

4. Adding the design option state objects, actions, and events.

5. Adding the colour buttons, actions, and events.

6. Adding the T-shirt option state objects, actions, and events

7. Adding the page change state objects.

8. Exporting the project.

Setting up the project and basic layout

For our sample site, we created a custom page layout, but you can choose any page size you prefer.

1 On the **File** menu, point to **New**, then click **New Keyframe Animation**.

2 On the Page context toolbar, in the Page size drop-down list, click **Custom**.

In the **Keyframe Animation Page Setup** dialog:

- In the **Width** box, enter 768 pixels.

- In the **Height** box, enter 704 pixels.

- Select the **Wide** option button.

- Click **OK**.

Add Animation to a Web Site

We'll now construct the basic layout and main page elements of our Web page.

3 On the Drawing toolbar, on the Quick Shapes flyout, use the ▢ **Quick Rectangle** to create four main areas on your page. The following exploded diagram describes how we created our page elements, but feel free to use your own favourite tools and techniques.

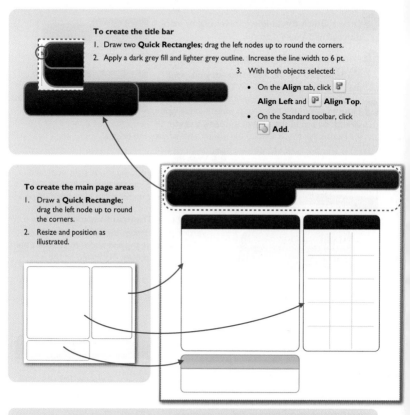

To create the title bar

1. Draw two **Quick Rectangles**; drag the left nodes up to round the corners.

2. Apply a dark grey fill and lighter grey outline. Increase the line width to 6 pt.

3. With both objects selected:

   - On the **Align** tab, click ▣ **Align Left** and ▣ **Align Top**.

   - On the Standard toolbar, click ▣ **Add**.

To create the main page areas

1. Draw a **Quick Rectangle**; drag the left node up to round the corners.

2. Resize and position as illustrated.

To create the section header bars

1. Draw a **Quick Rectangle**; drag the left node up to round the corners. Apply a colour of your choice.

2. On the Standard toolbar, click ⟳ **Convert to Curves** and then click the ▷ **Node** tool.

3. Drag a selection bounding box around the lower two nodes and press **Delete**.

Add Animation to a Web Site

Now we'll create the **Designs** and **T-Shirts** buttons and grid.

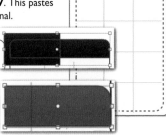

4 Use the ╲ **Straight Line** tool to construct a 3 x 5 grid. Apply the colour of your choice.

5 Select the header bar. Click **Ctrl + C** then **Ctrl + V**. This pastes a copy of the header bar directly on top of the original.

6 Draw a **Quick Rectangle** to cover slightly more than half of the new shape.

7 Select both shapes. On the Standard toolbar, click ⬚ **Subtract**. On the **Transparency** tab, apply the **78% Opacity** swatch.

8 Make a copy of the new shape; leave it in position directly on top of the original and apply a white fill. Resize this shape so that it is slightly smaller than the original.

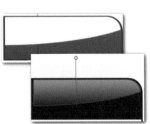

9 With the new shape selected, click the ▷ **Node** tool. Select the lower right node and click **Delete**. Drag the lower left node and curve segment up to create a rounded shape.

10 Click the ⬚ **Transparency** tool and draw a vertical path through the centre of the shape. Adjust the start and end nodes to achieve a gel effect similar to ours, illustrated on the left.

11 Select the two shapes, then right-click and click **Copy**. Right-click again and click **Paste**. On the Standard toolbar, click ⬚ **Flip Horizontal**.

12 Drag the copied shapes into position on the left side of the header bar. Click the **A** **Artistic Text** tool and add your button labels.

13 On the **Layers** tab, rename your buttons (the main shape, not the gel effect) 'DesignsButton' and 'ShirtsButton' so that you can find them later.

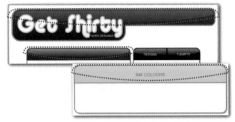

14 Repeat steps 9 to 10 to add gel effects to the title bar and the other two header bars.

15 Use the **A** **Artistic Text** tool to add a label to the 'ink colours' section at the bottom of the page, and to add the title for your Web page.

Add Animation to a Web Site

Your page should now look something like ours.

16 On the **Layers** tab, right click Layer 1.

In the **Layer Properties** dialog, rename this layer 'Basic elements.'

> 💡 When working on complex multi-layered documents, it's always a good idea to name your layers appropriately.

Creating the t-shirt style options and mask

In this section, we'll create our t-shirt styles and mask.

To create the t-shirt styles group

1 On the **Layers** tab, click ➕ **Add**. Name this layer 'Tshirt styles.'

2 Use your preferred drawing tool (we used the **Pen** tool) to draw your first T-shirt style in the large square pane. Select all of the curve segments that make up your drawing and click the ▦ **Group** button.

3 Select your t-shirt group, then on the **Tools** menu, click **Replicate**.

4 In the **Replicate** dialog:

- In the **Columns** box, enter **3**.

- In the **Rows** box, enter **5**.

- In both the **X Spacing** and **Y Spacing** boxes, enter **80 pixels**.

DrawPlus fills a 3 x 5 grid with identical copies of the t-shirt.

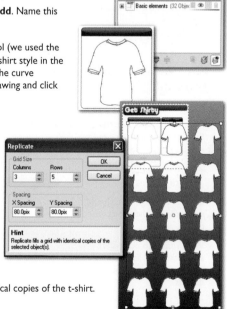

Replicate dialog:

Grid Size
Columns: 3
Rows: 5
[OK] [Cancel]

Spacing
X Spacing: 80.0pix
Y Spacing: 80.0pix

Hint
Replicate fills a grid with identical copies of the selected object(s).

Add Animation to a Web Site

5 Select each t-shirt group in turn, ungroup it, and make changes to the style and colour as required.

(You'll need to move the whole group up to work on the bottom few rows.)

6 When you've made your changes, regroup each style, and then regroup the whole set of styles.

On the **Layers** tab, name the main t-shirt group 'ShirtsGroup.'

Now we'll create our first mask. This will hide all of the t-shirt styles, except for the one that is displayed in the main viewing pane.

To create the mask

1 On the **Layers** tab, click ✛ **Add**. Name this layer 'Mask shirts.'

2 Draw a ▢ **Quick Rectangle** to cover the t-shirt style in the main pane. Apply a bright fill.

💡 It doesn't matter what colour you choose for your mask as it won't be seen in the final animation. However, when working with masks, it's generally a good idea to make them bright and easily identifiable (especially when working on complex projects like this one).

3 On the **Layers** tab, to the right of your mask layer, click the 🅼 **Mask** and 🔒 **Lock** buttons.

Back on the page, you should now only see the t-shirt inside the main pane.

We'll return to our t-shirt styles later, but for now let's move on and create our designs.

Creating the design options and mask

In this section, we'll create and mask a selection of designs for our t-shirts.

To create the design options group

1. On the **Layers** tab, click ✚ **Add**. Name this layer 'Design styles.'

2. Add your first design to the t-shirt displayed in the main pane. We've dragged items directly from the **Gallery** tab, but you can be as creative as you want.

3. Create a 3 x 5 grid of designs; use the **Align** tab to align them in evenly spaced, centred rows and columns.

4. Select all of the designs and then click ▦ **Group**.

5. On the **Transform** tab, drag the blue anchor point to the upper left position. The X and Y boxes now display the horizontal and vertical position of the top left corner of your design group. Make a note of these coordinates as you'll need them again later.

6. On the **Layers** tab, name your group **DesignGroup**.

Now we'll create our second mask. This one will hide all of the designs, except for the one that is displayed in the main viewing pane.

To create the mask

1. On the **Layers** tab, click ✚ **Add**. Name this layer 'Mask designs.'

2. Draw a ◯ **Quick Ellipse** to cover the design in the main pane of the page. Apply a bright fill.

3. On the **Layers** tab, to the right of your mask layer, click the Ⓜ **Mask** and 🔒 **Lock** buttons.

   Back on the page, you should now only see the design that is positioned on the t-shirt.

Our next task is to create option buttons to allow users to choose the design they want to print on their t-shirt.

Add Animation to a Web Site

Adding the design option buttons, actions, and events

In this section, we'll add the design option buttons to the grid we created on the right of the page. We'll also use **state objects** to change the colour of the buttons when the user hovers over them.

1 On the **Layers** tab, click ✛ **Add**. Name this layer 'Option Button Images.'

2 On the **Layers** tab, click to clear the **Mask designs** 🔒 **Lock** button and display the whole design group.

3 On the **Designs styles** layer, select the design group and press **Ctrl + C** to place a copy onto the Clipboard.

4 On the **Layers** tab, click to reselect the **Mask designs** 🔒 **Lock** button and hide the design group.

5 On your new **Option Button Images** layer, press **Ctrl + V** to paste a copy of the design group onto the page.

Resize and position the group so that it fits inside the grid.

Great, we have the images for our design buttons; now we need to create and program the buttons that are activated when users select a design.

6 On the **Layers** tab, click ✛ **Add**. Name this layer 'Options.'

7 Draw a ▢ **Quick Rectangle** to fit inside the upper left square of the grid.

8 With the square selected, on the **Object** menu, choose **State** and then click **Convert to state object**.

You'll now see two buttons displayed next to the shape.

These buttons allow us to change the attributes of the object when the user hovers over or presses the object.

9 Press the 🔘 **Hover** button. On the **Swatches** or **Colour** tab, apply a fill colour of your choice.

10 On the **Storyboard** tab, in the ▶ ▾ **Preview** drop-down list, click **Preview in Flash Player**.

Hover over the upper left square of the grid to see the fill colour applied.

You may have noticed that the design does display in this square. This is because it is on the layer beneath the filled square. We can easily correct this by changing the layer order.

11 On the **Layers** tab, select the **Options** layer and click ▼ **Move Layer Down** to move this layer below the **Option Button Images** layer.

Preview your animation again and you'll see that the design now shows on top of the filled square.

12 Copy and paste your state object into each section of the grid.

We now have the 'hover over' behaviour we require.

Our next task is to change the displayed design to match the option chosen by the user. To do this we need to move our **Design Group** object so that the chosen design is centred under the mask. We'll use the **Actions** tab to achieve this.

13 Select the upper left state object square, then on the **Actions** tab, double-click the **Mouse Release (Object)** event (or click ⚙ **Edit**).

In the **Mouse Release (Object)** dialog:

- Expand the **Position Actions** category and the **Other Objects** subcategory.

- In the **Other Objects** list, double-click **Set position of object X**.

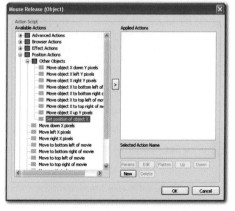

14 In the **Set position of object X Parameters** dialog:

- In the drop-down **Object** list, select **DesignGroup**.

- In the **X** and **Y** boxes, enter the design group X and Y coordinates you noted earlier.

- Click **OK** to close the dialog.

15 Back in the **Mouse Release (Object)** dialog, your new action is listed in the **Applied Actions** pane. Click **OK** to close the dialog.

> To adjust the parameters (the X and Y coordinates) of this action later, simply select the action in the **Applied Actions** pane and then click **Params** to redisplay the **Set position of object X Parameters** dialog.

16 On the **Layers** tab, on the **Mask Design**s layer, click to clear the 🅼 **Mask** button and display the entire design group. Click to select the **Design styles** layer.

17 On the **Design styles** layer, drag the group so that the next design in the row is centred under the mask. (As soon as you release the mouse button, the image will be masked.)

On the **Transform** tab, make a note of the new X and Y coordinates.

18 On the **Layers** tab, return to the **Options** layer. In the options grid, select the state object square that corresponds to the image you just positioned. On the **Actions** tab, double-click the **Mouse Release (Object)** event.

In the **Mouse Release (Object)** dialog:

- Expand the **Position Actions** category and the **Other Objects** subcategory.

- In the **Other Objects** list, double-click **Set position of object X**.

19 In the **Set position of object X Parameters** dialog:

- In the drop-down **Object** list, select **DesignGroup**.

- In the **X** and **Y** value boxes, enter the X and Y coordinates you noted in step 17.

- Click **OK** to close the dialog.

20 Preview your animation again. Click between the two design buttons to see the results of your work.

21 Repeat steps 17 to 19 to set the position of the design group when each of the remaining state objects is clicked.

When you've completed this task, click to select the **M** **Mask** button on the **Mask Designs** layer to hide the design group once again.

Great, our users can click to change the design for their t-shirts, but what if they also want to change the colour. The following section will show you how to do this.

Adding the colour buttons, actions, and events.

1 On the **Layers** tab, select the **Option Button Images** layer, then click **Add**. Name the new layer 'Colour options.'

2 At the bottom of the page, in the Ink Colours section, create a series of **Quick Rectangles**.

- Apply a different fill colour to each shape.

- Apply a grey outline to each shape.

3 With the first colour swatch selected:

- On the **Object** menu, choose **State** and then click **Convert to state object**.

- Click the **Hover** button and change the outline colour to black.

4 With the swatch still selected, on the **Colour** tab, click the **Fill** swatch to display the HSL values.

5 On the **Actions** tab, double-click the **Mouse Release (Object)** event. In the **Mouse Release (Object)** dialog:

- Expand the **Effect Actions** category and the **Other Objects** subcategory.

- In the **Other Objects** list, double-click **Recolour object X**.

6 In the **Recolour object X Parameters** dialog, in the drop-down **Object** list, select **DesignGroup** and then click the **Colour** bar to open the **Colour Picker**.

- In the **Model** drop-down list, select **HSL Sliders**.

- In the **H**, **S**, and **L** boxes, enter the values displayed on the **Colour** tab and click **OK**.

Add Animation to a Web Site

7 In the **Recolour object X Parameters** dialog, the **Colour** bar is updated. Click **OK** to accept the new colour and close the dialog.

8 In the **Mouse Release (Object)** dialog, the **Recolour object X** action is displayed in the **Applied Actions** pane. Click **OK** to close the dialog.

9 Preview your animation. Click the first ink colour swatch to change design colour.

10 Selecting each of the colour swatches in turn, repeat steps 3 to 8 to convert them to state objects and assign the appropriate recolour action.

We've completed the design and colour options for our Web site. Now we need to provide a way for our users to choose a t-shirt style.

Adding the T-shirt style state objects, actions, and events

In our first (and currently our only) keyframe, we added the design option buttons to the grid on the right of the page. We'll use this same grid for our t-shirt style options and let users switch between the shirt style and design options by clicking the 'T-Shirts' and 'Designs' buttons.

To do this, we'll need to create our t-shirt style buttons on a second keyframe.

1 On the **Storyboard** tab, click ▣ **Insert**.

2 In the **Insert Keyframes** dialog, accept the default values and click **OK**.

3 DrawPlus adds a second keyframe to the **Storyboard** tab.

By default, this keyframe contains all of the elements you created on keyframe 1.

4 Click the ▽ **Marker** arrowhead that sits between the two keyframes. In the **Marker** dialog:

- Name the marker 'Tshirts.'

- Select the **Stops playhead** check box.

On the **Storyboard** tab, the new marker is indicated with a 'selected' icon and a vertical red line. We'll come back to this later in the section.

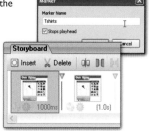

Add Animation to a Web Site

5 On the **Storyboard** tab, click on the new keyframe to open it in the workspace.

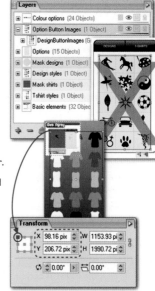

6 On the **Layers** tab, click the **Option Button Images** layer.

On the page. select the group containing your design images and press **Delete**.

7 On the **Layers** tab, click to clear the M **Mask** button next to the **Mask shirts** layer to display the entire t-shirt style group.

8 On the **Layers** tab, click the **T-shirt styles** layer.

Select the group containing your t-shirt styles and then press **Ctrl + C** to copy it to the Clipboard.

9 On the **Transform** tab, drag the blue anchor point to the upper left position.

The X and Y boxes display the horizontal and vertical position of the top left corner of your t-shirt style group. Make a note of these values.

10 On the **Layers** tab, click the ◉ **Hide** button next to the **T-shirt styles** layer to temporarily hide this layer.

11 On the **Layers** tab, click the **Option Button Images** layer.

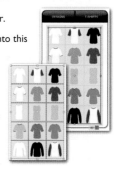

Press **Ctrl + V** to paste a copy of the t-shirt styles group onto this layer. Resize and position the group to fit inside the grid.

12 On **keyframe 1**, on the **Options** layer, press **Ctrl + A** to select all of the state object squares, then on the **Run** menu, click **Break**.

We can now edit the actions for these buttons on keyframe 2, without affecting the actions added in our first keyframe.

13 On **keyframe 2**, on the **Options** layer, select the first state object square and on the **Actions** tab, double-click the **Mouse Release (Object)** event (or click ⚙ **Edit**).

14 In the **Mouse Release (Object)** dialog, in the **Applied Actions** pane, select the **Set position of object X** action and click the **Params** button.

15 In the **Set position of object X Parameters** dialog,

- In the **Object** drop-down list, select **ShirtsGroup**.
- In the **X** and **Y** boxes, enter the X and Y values you noted in step 9 and click **OK**.

Add Animation to a Web Site

16 Click **OK** to close the **Mouse Release (Object)** dialog.

17 On the **Layers** tab, click the 👁 **Show** button next to the **T-shirt styles** layer to redisplay this layer.

18 Back on the **T-shirt styles** layer, drag the group so that the next t-shirt style in the row is centred under the mask.

On the **Transform** tab, make a note of the new X and Y coordinates.

19 On the **Layers** tab, return to the **Options** layer. In the options grid, select the state object square that corresponds to the t-shirt style you just positioned.

On the **Actions** tab, double-click the **Mouse Release (Object)** event.

20 In the **Mouse Release (Object)** dialog:

- In the **Applied Actions** pane, select the **Set position of object X** action and click the **Params** button.

In the **Set position of object X Parameters** dialog:

- In the **Object** drop-down list, select **ShirtsGroup**.

- In the **X** and **Y** boxes, enter the X and Y coordinates you noted in step 18.

- Click **OK** to close the dialogs.

21 Repeat steps 18 to 20 to set the position of the t-shirt styles group when each of the remaining state objects is clicked.

When you've completed this task, click to select the ⓜ **Mask** button on the **Mask shirts** layer to mask the entire t-shirt style group once again.

To see our t-shirt style options in action, we need to add actions to the Designs and T-Shirts buttons, to allow users to switch between the design and t-shirts pages.

Adding the page change state objects
In this last section, we'll convert the Designs and T-Shirts buttons to state objects, then we'll add the required actions.

1 On the **Storyboard** tab, click the first keyframe.

2 On the **Layers** tab, select the **Basic elements** layer and click to expand the layer.

- Scroll down the list of objects and click on the **ShirtsButton** object to select it on the page.

3 On the **Object** menu, choose **State** and then click **Convert to state object**.

4 Press the ▶ **Hover** button.

Click the ◈ **Fill** tool and drag a vertical fill path through the button. Apply a grey-to-white-to-grey linear fill, as illustrated.

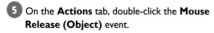

5 On the **Actions** tab, double-click the **Mouse Release (Object)** event.

- In the **Mouse Release (Object)** dialog, expand the **Timeline Actions** category and double-click **Goto marker X and stop**.

- In the **Goto marker X and stop Parameters** dialog, in the **Marker** drop-down list, select **Tshirts** and click **OK**.

- Click **OK** to close the **Mouse Release (Object)** dialog.

6 With the **ShirtsButton** state object selected, on the **Run** menu, click **Break**.

7 In **keyframe 2**, we don't need to assign any action to the **ShirtsButton** state object so let's remove it—to do so, select the object and then on the **Actions** tab, click ⊗ **Clear** to remove the **Mouse Release (Object)** event.

8 Still working on the second keyframe, select the **DesignsButton** object.

In this keyframe, when the user clicks the Designs button, we want to return to the previous keyframe and display the design options in the grid.

9 Repeat steps 3 and 4 to convert the **DesignsButton** object to a state object and add a gradient fill.

10 On the **Actions** tab, double-click the **Mouse Release (Object)** event.

- In the **Mouse Release (Object)** dialog, expand the **Timeline Actions** category and double-click **Rewind movie X frames**.

- In the **Rewind movie X frames** dialog, in the **Frames** box, enter **1** and click **OK**.

- Click **OK** to close the **Mouse Release (Object)** dialog.

11 On the **Storyboard** tab, return to **keyframe 1**. Select the same **DesignsButton** state object, then on the **Run** menu, click **Break**.

Add Animation to a Web Site

12 On the **Actions** tab, click ⊗ **Clear** to remove the **Mouse Release (Object)** event for the **DesignsButton** state object.

13 Preview your project. Click the Designs and T-shirts buttons to switch between the design and t-shirt style pages.

We've now completed all of the elements we wanted to include in our project and we're ready to export it.

You can include additional elements on your pages—for example, a decorative background (create this on a separate layer and move it right to the bottom of the **Layers** tab), additional buttons, or even additional keyframes if you want to challenge yourself!

Exporting the project

We'll export our project to Adobe® Shockwave Flash® (SWF) format.

1 On the **File** menu, choose **Export** and then click **Export as Flash SWF**.

2 Choose a file name and save location for your .swf file and then click **Save**.

3 When export is complete, browse to locate the file and then double-click to open it.

Congratulations, you've completed the project! This has been a more challenging exercise, but we hope that you have learned a lot from it and are happy with the results.

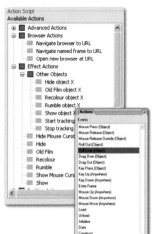

It's worth noting that in our example, we only used:

- One event—**Mouse Release (Object)**

- One Position action—**Set position of object X**

- One Effect action—**Recolour object X**

- Two Timeline actions—**Goto marker X** and **Rewind movie X frames**

However, the **Actions** tab provides a wide range of preset events and actions from which to choose. We hope you'll enjoy experimenting with them in your own animation projects.

DrawPlus
Gallery

2

Introduction

DrawPlus Gallery

This chapter lists the content items provided within the **DrawPlus X2 Gallery**, from **Arts & Crafts**, **Cartoons**, **Connecting Symbols**, **Curriculum**, **Layout Symbols** to **Shape Art**.

These can be found on the **Program CD** and the **Resource CD**.

Note: The **Business** section and the **Technical** category in the **Layout Symbols** section are not available in this Resource Guide.

Arts & Crafts - Alphabet / Badges

Arts & Crafts

A
**Alphabet
A**

B
**Alphabet
B**

C
**Alphabet
C**

D
**Alphabet
D**

E
**Alphabet
E**

F
**Alphabet
F**

G
**Alphabet
G**

H
**Alphabet
H**

I
**Alphabet
I**

J
**Alphabet
J**

K
**Alphabet
K**

L
**Alphabet
L**

M
**Alphabet
M**

N
**Alphabet
N**

O
**Alphabet
O**

P
**Alphabet
P**

Q
**Alphabet
Q**

R
**Alphabet
R**

S
**Alphabet
S**

T
**Alphabet
T**

U
**Alphabet
U**

V
**Alphabet
V**

W
**Alphabet
W**

X
**Alphabet
X**

Y
**Alphabet
Y**

Z
**Alphabet
Z**

Arts & Crafts - Badges / Scrapbooking

Badges
Boy

Badges
Butterflies

Badges
Car

Badges
Dice

Badges
Fire

Badges
Flaming Bike

Badges
Flower

Badges
Girl

Badges
I Love You

Badges
Mod

Badges
Pop

Badges
Punk

Badges
Rainbow

Badges
Rock

Badges
Seal

Badges
Skull

Badges
Smile

Badges
Star

Scrapbooking
Boggly Eyes

Scrapbooking
Buttons

Scrapbooking
Flower Beads

Scrapbooking
Furry Dogs

Scrapbooking
Furry Flowers

Scrapbooking
Furry Sun

Scrapbooking
Furry Teddies

Scrapbooking
Glass Beads

Scrapbooking
Jewels

Scrapbooking
Label

Arts & Crafts - Scrapbooking / Printmaking

Scrapbooking
Note

Scrapbooking
Old Label

Scrapbooking
Page Corner

Scrapbooking
Page Curl

Scrapbooking
Paper

Scrapbooking
Paper

Scrapbooking
Paper Clip

Scrapbooking
Pin

Scrapbooking
Pin

Scrapbooking
Pin

Scrapbooking
Pink Note

Scrapbooking
Polaroid

Scrapbooking
Price

Scrapbooking
Price

Scrapbooking
Safety Pins

Scrapbooking
Sequins

Scrapbooking
Sticker

Scrapbooking
Tag

Scrapbooking
Tag

Scrapbooking
Tape Measure

Scrapbooking
Yellow Note

Scrapbooking
Yellow Note

Printmaking
Bird 2

Printmaking
Brid 1

Printmaking
Coffee 1

Printmaking
Coffee 2

Printmaking
Coffee 3

Arts & Crafts - Printmaking / Stickers

Printmaking
Coffee 4

Printmaking
Coffee 5

Printmaking
Coffee 6

Printmaking
Feet

Printmaking
Grass I

Printmaking
Grass 2

Printmaking
Grass 3

Printmaking
Hand

Printmaking
Lips I

Printmaking
Lips 2

Printmaking
Paws I

Printmaking
Paws 2

Printmaking
Splatt I

Printmaking
Splatt 2

Printmaking
Splatt 3

Printmaking
Tea

Printmaking
Wine

Stickers
Blue Cat

Stickers
Blue Radio

Stickers
Blue Stars 2

Stickers
Blue Stars

Stickers
Cherry Cream

Stickers
Golden Rabbit

Stickers
Ice Cream

Stickers
Marino Cherry

Stickers
Mint Sweets

Stickers
Moon Light
Cocktail

Arts & Crafts - Stickers / Tattoos / Vectors

Stickers
Orange Cat

Stickers
Orange Sweets

Stickers
Party Cat

Stickers
Party Rabbit

Stickers
Raspberry Cat

Stickers
Raspberry Radio

Stickers
Red Rabbit

Stickers
Star Cherry

Stickers
Strawberry
Cream

Stickers
Sun Cocktail

Stickers
Sunset Cocktail

Stickers
Vanilla Cherry

Stickers
Vanilla Cream

Stickers
White Rabbit

Tattoos
Celtan

Tattoos
Crom

Tattoos
Gekkoz

Tattoos
Kung Fu

Tattoos
Mountain Goat

Tattoos
Pistolero

Tattoos
Smoking Gun

Tattoos
Spore

Tattoos
Squid

Tattoos
The Blade

Tattoos
Vision Quest

Tattoos
Warrior

Arts & Crafts - Vectors

Vectors
Aeroplane

Vectors
Branch01

Vectors
Branch02

Vectors
Branch03

Vectors
Branch04

Vectors
Branch05

Vectors
Branch06

Vectors
Branch07

Vectors
Branch08

Vectors
Branch09

Vectors
Branch10

Vectors
Branch11

Vectors
Branch12

Vectors
Branch13

Vectors
Branch14

Vectors
Branch15

Vectors
Branch16

Vectors
Car

Vectors
Decorative01

Vectors
Decorative02

Vectors
Decorative03

Vectors
Decorative04

Vectors
Decorative05

Vectors
Decorative06

Vectors
Decorative07

Vectors
Floral01

Vectors
Floral02

Vectors
Floral03

Vectors
Floral04

Vectors
Floral05

Arts & Crafts - Vectors

Vectors
Floral06

Vectors
Floral07

Vectors
Floral08

Vectors
Floral09

Vectors
Floral10

Vectors
Floral11

Vectors
Motif01

Vectors
Motif02

Vectors
Motif03

Vectors
Motif04

Vectors
Motif05

Vectors
Motif06

Vectors
Motif07

Vectors
Motif08

Vectors
Motif09

Vectors
Motif10

Vectors
Pop01

Vectors
Pop02

Vectors
Pop03

Vectors
Pop04

Vectors
Pop05

Vectors
Pop06

Vectors
Pop07

Vectors
Pop08

Vectors
Pop09

Vectors
Pop10

Vectors
Pop11

Vectors
Pop12

Vectors
Pop13

Vectors
Scatter01

Arts & Crafts - Vectors

Vectors
Scatter02

Vectors
Scatter03

Vectors
Scatter04

Vectors
Scatter05

Vectors
Scatter06

Vectors
Scatter07

Vectors
Scatter08

Vectors
Scatter09

Vectors
Scatter10

Vectors
Scatter11

Vectors
Twirl01

Vectors
Twirl02

Vectors
Twirl03

Vectors
Twirl04

Vectors
Twirl05

Vectors
Twirl06

Vectors
Twirl07

Vectors
Twirl08

Vectors
Twirl09

Vectors
Twirl10

Vectors
Twirl11

Vectors
Twirl12

Vectors
Twirl13

Vectors
Twirl14

Vectors
Twirl15

Vectors
Twirl16

Vectors
Twirl17

Vectors
Twirl18

Vectors
Twirl19

Vectors
Twirl20

Vectors
Twirl21

Vectors
Twirl22

Vectors
Twirl23

Cartoons - Artistic

Animals
Bird

Animals
Bumblebee

Animals
Cat

Animals
Cow

Animals
Crab

Animals
Crocodile

Animals
Dinosaur -
Brontosaurus

Animals
Dog

Animals
Donkey

Animals
Dove

Animals
Eagle

Animals
Elephant

Animals
Frog

Animals
Giraffe

Animals
Goldfish

Animals
Hamster

Animals
Hedgehog

Animals
Hippopotamus

Animals
Horse

Animals
Killer Whale

Animals
Ladybird

Animals
Lion

Animals
Lizard

Animals
Mouse

Animals
Owl Baby

Cartoons - Artistic

Animals
Owl

Animals
Penguin

Animals
Pig

Animals
Rabbit

Animals
Rat

Animals
Rhinoceros

Animals
Rooster

Animals
Shark

Animals
Sheep

Animals
Snake

Animals
Spider

Animals
Starfish

Animals
Tiger

Animals
Whale

Birth
Baby Mobile

Birth
Baby Bottle

Birth
Baby

Birth
Bib for Boy

Birth
Bib for Girl

Birth
Bootie

Birth
Bottle

Birth
Boy Girl Symbol

Birth
Boy's Baby
Rattle

Birth
Boy's Booties

Birth
Butterfly

Cartoons - Artistic

Birth
Flower

Birth
Girl's Baby
Rattle

Birth
Girl's Booties

Birth
Moon

Birth
Pacifier

Birth
Rattle

Birth
Rocking Bed

Birth
Romper Suit

Birth
Sock

Birth
Star

Birth
Stork for Boy

Birth
Stork for Girl

Birth
Teddy Bear

Birth
Teddy

**Chinese
Calligraphy**
Ai - Love

**Chinese
Calligraphy**
Cai - Wealth

**Chinese
Calligraphy**
Fu - Good Luck

**Chinese
Calligraphy**
He -
Harmonious

**Chinese
Calligraphy**
Lu - Prosperity

**Chinese
Calligraphy**
Shou - Longevity

**Chinese
Calligraphy**
Xi - Happiness

Christmas
Angel

Christmas
Angel 02

Christmas
Baby Jesus

Christmas
Bauble

Cartoons - Artistic

Christmas
Bell

Christmas
Candle

Christmas
Candy Cane

Christmas
Christmas Tree

Christmas
Christmas Trees

Christmas
Cracker

Christmas
Crown

Christmas
Decorated
Christmas Tree

Christmas
Elf

Christmas
Fairy

Christmas
Gift

Christmas
Holly 02

Christmas
Holly 03

Christmas
Holly

Christmas
Mistletoe 01

Christmas
Mistletoe

Christmas
More Christmas
Trees

Christmas
Orange Bauble
1

Christmas
Orange Bauble
2

Christmas
Penguin Fairy

Christmas
Penguin on Tree

Christmas
Penguin with
Balloons

Christmas
Penguin with
Cake

Christmas
Penguin with
Party Hat

Christmas
Penguins and
Tinsel

Cartoons - Artistic

Christmas
Polar Bear

Christmas
Pudding

Christmas
Purple Bauble 1

Christmas
Purple Bauble 2

Christmas
Purple Present

Christmas
Red Present

Christmas
Reindeer

Christmas
Robin 02

Christmas
Robin

Christmas
Rudolph 2

Christmas
Rudolph

Christmas
Santa with Sack
of Presents

Christmas
Santa

Christmas
Scroll Banner

Christmas
Shepherd

Christmas
Simple Tree

Christmas
Snowman

Christmas
Stocking

Christmas
Stocking 02

Christmas
Sugar Cane

Christmas
Wise Man

Christmas
Wreath

Christmas
Wreath

Easter
Easter Bunny

Cartoons - Artistic

Easter
Easter Duckling

Easter
Egg Basket

Easter
Flowers

Fashion
Bathtime

Fashion
Boots

Fashion
Brush

Fashion
Champagne
Bottle

Fashion
Champagne
Glasses

Fashion
Eyelash Brush

Fashion
Flowers in Vase

Fashion
Flowers

Fashion
Gold Perfume
Bottle

Fashion
Green Perfume
Bottle

Fashion
Hair Brush

Fashion
Hairdryer

Fashion
Handbag

Fashion
Hat

Fashion
High Heels

Fashion
Lipstick

Fashion
Make-Up Brush

Fashion
Mirror 1

Fashion
Mirror 2

Fashion
Perfume

Fashion
Platform Shoes

Fashion
Shoes

Cartoons - Artistic

Fashion
Shopping Girl

Fashion
Slippers

Fashion
Spray

Fashion
Star

Funny Faces
Angry Eyes

Funny Faces
Army Helmet

Funny Faces
Baby Bonnet

Funny Faces
Blood-shot Eyes

Funny Faces
Brown Beard

Funny Faces
Cowboy
Bandana

Funny Faces
Cowboy Hat

Funny Faces
Cute Eyes

Funny Faces
Dracula

Funny Faces
Ear Warmers

Funny Faces
Ears

Funny Faces
Elf Ears

Funny Faces
Elf Hat

Funny Faces
Frankenstein
Bolts

Funny Faces
Frankenstein

Funny Faces
Hairdo 1

Funny Faces
Hairdo 2

Funny Faces
Hairdo 3

Funny Faces
Hairdo 4

Funny Faces
Lazy Eyes

Funny Faces
Hypnotic Eyes

Cartoons - Artistic

Funny Faces
Mexican Hat

Funny Faces
Mexican
Moustache

Funny Faces
Native Indian
Hairdo

Funny Faces
Native Indian
Headdress

Funny Faces
Nose 1

Funny Faces
Nose 2

Funny Faces
Nose 3

Funny Faces
Pioneer

Funny Faces
Pirate Hat and
Eye Patch

Funny Faces
Pirate's Parrot

Funny Faces
Purple Beard

Funny Faces
Sailors Hat

Funny Faces
Scary Mouth 1

Funny Faces
Scary Mouth 2

Funny Faces
Scary Mouth 3

Funny Faces
Sheriff Badge

Funny Faces
Silly Mouth 1

Gardening
Fork

Gardening
Hand Fork

Gardening
Mower

Gardening
Plant Pot

Gardening
Pruner

Gardening
Rake

Gardening
Spade

Gardening
Trowel

Cartoons - Artistic

Nature and Seasons
Clouds

Nature and Seasons
Glove

Nature and Seasons
Grass

Nature and Seasons
Hat

Nature and Seasons
Kite

Nature and Seasons
Leaf

Nature and Seasons
Rainbow

Nature and Seasons
Scarf

Nature and Seasons
Snowflake

Nature and Seasons
Storm

Nature and Seasons
Sun

Nature and Seasons
Sunflower

Nature and Seasons
Tree

Nature and Seasons
Umbrella

Nature and Seasons
Wellies

Party
Balloon

Party
Bottle Cork

Party
Champagne

Party
Cupcake

Party
Party Blower

Party
Party Hat

Party
Party Popper

People
Boy

People
Builder

People
Businessman

Cartoons - Artistic

People
Chef

People
Fireman

People
Girl

People
Nurse

People
Policeman

People
Spaceman

People
Teacher

Romance
Cake

Romance
Cat

Romance
Cupid

Romance
Flower Cluster

Romance
Heart 1

Romance
Heart 2

Romance
Heart 3

Romance
Heart with Stars

Romance
Heart

Romance
Hearts

Romance
Honey Bear 2

Romance
Honey Bear

Romance
New York
Couple

Romance
Painted Rose

Romance
Purple Flowers

Romance
Rose

Romance
Wedding
Figures

Transport
Boat

Cartoons - Artistic

Transport
Bus

Transport
Car 01

Transport
Car 02

Transport
Forklift Truck

Transport
Jet

Transport
Scooter

Transport
Truck

Wedding
Bells

Wedding
Bouquet

Wedding
Bride

Wedding
Bridesmaid
Dress

Wedding
Cake

Wedding
Church

Wedding
Dress

Wedding
Garter

Wedding
Groom

Wedding
Horseshoe

Wedding
Just Married
Sign

Wedding
Limousine

Wedding
Top Hat

Zodiac Signs
Aquarius

Zodiac Signs
Aries

Zodiac Signs
Cancer

Zodiac Signs
Capricorn

Zodiac Signs
Gemini

Cartoons - Artistic / Colour

Zodiac Signs
Leo

Zodiac Signs
Libra

Zodiac Signs
Pisces

Zodiac Signs
Sagittarius

Zodiac Signs
Scorpio

Zodiac Signs
Taurus

Zodiac Signs
Virgo

Cartoons - Colour

Animals
Bird

Animals
Bumblebee

Animals
Cow

Animals
Crab

Animals
Crocodile

Animals
Dinosaur -
Brontosaurus

Animals
Dog

Animals
Donkey

Animals
Dove

Animals
Eagle

Animals
Elephant

Animals
Hampster

Animals
Frog

Animals
Giraffe

Animals
Goldfish

Cartoons - Colour

Animals
Hedgehog

Animals
Hippopotamus

Animals
Horse

Animals
Killer Whale

Animals
Ladybird

Animals
Lion

Animals
Lizard

Animals
Monkey

Animals
Mouse

Animals
Owl Baby

Animals
Owl

Animals
Penguin

Animals
Pig

Animals
Rabbit

Animals
Rat

Animals
Rhinoceros

Animals
Rooster

Animals
Shark

Animals
Sheep

Animals
Snake

Animals
Spider

Animals
Starfish

Animals
Tiger

Animals
Whale

Birth
Baby

Cartoons - Colour

Birth
Bib for Boy

Birth
Bib for Girl

Birth
Bootie

Birth
Bottle

Birth
Boy Girl Symbol

Birth
Pacifier

Birth
Rattle

Birth
Romper Suit

Birth
Sock

Birth
Teddy

Buildings
Apartments 2

Buildings
Apartments

Buildings
Beach House

Buildings
Church

Buildings
Cottage

Buildings
Factory

Buildings
House

Buildings
Office

Buildings
Onion Towers

Buildings
Power Station

Buildings
Shack

Buildings
Shop

Buildings
The Clink

Buildings
Tower Block 2

Buildings
Tower Block 3

Cartoons - Colour

Buildings
Tower Block

Christmas
Angel 02

Christmas
Angel

Christmas
Baby Jesus

Christmas
Bauble

Christmas
Christmas
Pudding

Christmas
Christmas Tree

Christmas
Cracker

Christmas
Crown

Christmas
Holly

Christmas
Mistletoe

Christmas
Present

Christmas
Reindeer

Christmas
Robin

Christmas
Santa Claus

Christmas
Shepherd

Christmas
Snowman

Christmas
Stocking

Christmas
Sugar Cane

Christmas
Wise Man

Christmas
Wreath

Food & Drink
Apple

Food & Drink
Banana

Food & Drink
Beans on Toast

Food & Drink
Beefburger

Cartoons - Colour

Food & Drink
Beer

Food & Drink
Boiled Egg

Food & Drink
Bottle of Wine

Food & Drink
Bread

Food & Drink
Cake

Food & Drink
Carrot

Food & Drink
Cauliflower

Food & Drink
Cheese

Food & Drink
Chefs Hat

Food & Drink
Chicken Leg

Food & Drink
Chilli

Food & Drink
Croissant

Food & Drink
Fish n Chips

Food & Drink
Fish

Food & Drink
Fork

Food & Drink
French Fries

Food & Drink
Fried Egg

Food & Drink
Frying Pan

Food & Drink
Grapefruit

Food & Drink
Grapes

Food & Drink
Hotdog

Food & Drink
Ice Cream

Food & Drink
Juice

Food & Drink
Knife

Food & Drink
Lemon & Lime

Cartoons - Colour

Food & Drink
Milk Bottle

Food & Drink
Mug of Tea

Food & Drink
Mushroom

Food & Drink
Orange

Food & Drink
Pear

Food & Drink
Peas (in a pod)

Food & Drink
Pepper

Food & Drink
Pie

Food & Drink
Spirit

Food & Drink
Wine

Gardening
Fork

Gardening
Hand Fork

Gardening
Mower

Gardening
Plant Pot

Gardening
Pruner

Gardening
Rake

Gardening
Spade

Gardening
Trowel

Hobbies & Leisure
Archery

Hobbies & Leisure
Artist Palette

Hobbies & Leisure
Backpack

Hobbies & Leisure
Ballerina

Hobbies & Leisure
Boat

Hobbies & Leisure
Boxing Gloves

Hobbies & Leisure
Camera

Cartoons - Colour

**Hobbies &
Leisure**
Fishing Rod

**Hobbies &
Leisure**
Football

**Hobbies &
Leisure**
Footballer

**Hobbies &
Leisure**
Golf Bag

**Hobbies &
Leisure**
Horse Riding

**Hobbies &
Leisure**
Ice Skates

**Hobbies &
Leisure**
Karate

**Hobbies &
Leisure**
Skier

**Hobbies &
Leisure**
Snooker

**Hobbies &
Leisure**
Tennis

Holidays
Balloons

Holidays
Beachball

Holidays
Bucket and
Spade

Holidays
Cake

Holidays
Candle

Holidays
Cute Hearts

Holidays
Easter Egg

Holidays
Graduation

Holidays
Heart

Holidays
Present

Holidays
Pumpkin

Holidays
Witch Hat

Home
Hi-Fi

Home
Radio

Home
Screwdriver 01

Cartoons - Colour

Home
Screwdriver 02

Home
Screwdriver 03

Home
Screwdriver 04

Home
Spanner

Home
Speaker

Home
TV

Misc
American
Football

Misc
Autumn
Background

Misc
Beach Ball

Misc
Bells 01

Misc
Brown Leaf

Misc
Car 02

Misc
Cat 02

Misc
Chopper

Misc
Clouds

Misc
Cogs

Misc
Easter Chick

Misc
Eggs

Misc
Fly

Misc
Flying Ant

Misc
Gear

Misc
Ghost

Misc
Graduation

Misc
Grass 01

Misc
Hammock

Cartoons - Colour

Misc
Hearts

Misc
Holly 01

Misc
Jet

Misc
Lizard

Misc
Melon

Misc
Motorcycle 02

Misc
Mountain Bike

Misc
Penguin

Misc
Pig

Misc
Pumpkin 01

Misc
Rabbit 02

Misc
Sandy
Background

Misc
Shark

Misc
Snowball Skier

Misc
Snowman

Misc
Speedo

Misc
Strawberry

Misc
Steering

Misc
Straw Bale

Misc
Summer
Background

Misc
Summer Daze

Misc
Sunny Cloud
Background

Misc
Tree

Misc
Wheelie

Music
Amp

Cartoons - Colour

Music
CD 01

Music
CD 02

Music
Cello

Music
Guitar

Music
Harp

Music
Keyboard

Music
Maracas

Music
mp3 Player

Nature and Seasons
Clouds

Nature and Seasons
Glove

Nature and Seasons
Grass

Nature and Seasons
Hat

Nature and Seasons
Kite

Nature and Seasons
Leaf

Nature and Seasons
Rainbow

Nature and Seasons
Scarf

Nature and Seasons
Snowflake

Nature and Seasons
Storm

Nature and Seasons
Sun

Nature and Seasons
Sunflower

Nature and Seasons
Tree

Nature and Seasons
Umbrella

Nature and Seasons
Wellies

Party
Balloon

Party
Balloons

Cartoons - Colour

Party
Bottle Cork

Party
Champagne

Party
Cupcake

Party
Party Blower

Party
Party Hat

Party
Party Popper

People
Boxer

People
Rugby Player

People
Sprite

People
Tennis Player

Professions
Butcher

Professions
Doctor

Professions
Fire Officer

Professions
Mechanic

Professions
Paramedic

Professions
Plumber

Professions
Police Officer

Professions
Postman

Transport
Boat

Transport
Bus

Transport
Car 01

Transport
Car 02

Transport
Forklift Truck

Transport
Jet

Transport
Scooter

Cartoons - Colour

Transport
Truck

Wedding
Bells

Wedding
Bouquet

Wedding
Bride

Wedding
Bridesmaid
Dress

Wedding
Cake

Wedding
Church

Wedding
Dress

Wedding
Garter

Wedding
Groom

Wedding
Horseshoe

Wedding
Just Married
Sign

Wedding
Limousine

Wedding
Top Hat

Cartoons - Silhouette

Birth
Baby

Birth
Bib

Birth
Bootie

Birth
Bottle

Birth
Pacifier

Birth
Rattle

Birth
Romper Suit

Birth
Sock

Birth
Teddy

Christmas
Bauble

Christmas
Christmas Pudding

Christmas
Christmas Tree

Christmas
Cracker

Christmas
Crown

Christmas
Holly

Christmas
Present

Christmas
Reindeer

Christmas
Robin

Christmas
Stocking

Christmas
Sugar Cane

Food & Drink
Apple

Food & Drink
Banana

Food & Drink
Beans on Toast

Food & Drink
Beefburger

Food & Drink
Beer

Cartoons - Silhouette

Food & Drink
Boiled Egg

Food & Drink
Bottle of Wine

Food & Drink
Bread

Food & Drink
Cake

Food & Drink
Carrot

Food & Drink
Cauliflower

Food & Drink
Cheese

Food & Drink
Chefs Hat

Food & Drink
Chicken Leg

Food & Drink
Chilli

Food & Drink
Croissant

Food & Drink
Fish n Chips

Food & Drink
Fish

Food & Drink
Fork

Food & Drink
French Fries

Food & Drink
Fried Egg

Food & Drink
Frying Pan

Food & Drink
Grapefruit

Food & Drink
Grapes

Food & Drink
Hotdog

Food & Drink
Ice Cream

Food & Drink
Juice

Food & Drink
Knife

Food & Drink
Lemon & Lime

Food & Drink
Milk Bottle

Cartoons - Silhouette

Food & Drink
Mug of Tea

Food & Drink
Mushroom

Food & Drink
Orange

Food & Drink
Pear

Food & Drink
Peas (in a pod)

Food & Drink
Pepper

Food & Drink
Pie

Food & Drink
Spirit

Food & Drink
Wine

Gardening
Fork

Gardening
Hand Fork

Gardening
Mower

Gardening
Plant Pot

Gardening
Pruner

Gardening
Rake

Gardening
Spade

Gardening
Trowel

Hobbies & Leisure
Archery

Hobbies & Leisure
Artist Palette

Hobbies & Leisure
Boat

Hobbies & Leisure
Camera

Hobbies & Leisure
Fishing Rod

Hobbies & Leisure
Football

Hobbies & Leisure
Footballer

Hobbies & Leisure
Horse Riding

Cartoons - Silhouette

**Hobbies &
Leisure**
Ice Skates

**Hobbies &
Leisure**
Karate

**Hobbies &
Leisure**
Rambler

**Hobbies &
Leisure**
Skier

Holidays
Balloons

Holidays
Bat

Holidays
Beachball

Holidays
Cake

Holidays
Candle

Holidays
Dove

Holidays
Easter Egg

Holidays
Ghost

Holidays
Graduation

Holidays
Present

Holidays
Pumpkin

Holidays
Sandcastle

Holidays
Witch Hat

Home
Hi-Fi

Home
Light Bulb 01

Home
Screwdriver 01

Home
Screwdriver 02

Home
Screwdriver 03

Home
Screwdriver 04

Home
Spanner

Misc
Bat

Cartoons - Silhouette

Misc
Beach
Background

Misc
Bells 02

Misc
Bicycle

Misc
Bodybuilder

Misc
Branch 01

Misc
Branch 02

Misc
Bug

Misc
Bunny Face

Misc
Butterfly

Misc
Car 01

Misc
Cat 01

Misc
Chess 01

Misc
Chess 02

Misc
Chess 03

Misc
Chilli

Misc
Christmas
Pudding

Misc
City Background

Misc
Dinner

Misc
Dog 01

Misc
Floral Shape

Misc
Flower 01

Misc
Flower 02

Misc
Football

Misc
Gorilla

Misc
Grass 02

Cartoons - Silhouette

Misc
Holly 02

Misc
Jogging

Misc
Leaf 01

Misc
Leaf 02

Misc
Leaf 03

Misc
Leaf 04

Misc
Leaves 01

Misc
Leaves 02

Misc
Lips

Misc
Male Female

Misc
Motorcycle 01

Misc
Motorcycle 03

Misc
Paw Print

Misc
Puppy Face

Misc
Ribbon

Misc
Running

Misc
Scorpion

Misc
Sheep Face

Misc
Snowflake 01

Misc
Snowflake 02

Misc
Stars

Misc
Sun 01

Misc
Sun 02

Misc
Tattoo 01

Misc
Tattoo 02

Cartoons - Silhouette

Misc
Yin Yang

Music
Acoustic Guitar

Music
Cello

Music
Drum Sticks

Music
Guitar

Music
Harp

Music
Maracas

Music
Violin

Nature and Seasons
Clouds

Nature and Seasons
Glove

Nature and Seasons
Grass

Nature and Seasons
Hat

Nature and Seasons
Kite

Nature and Seasons
Leaf

Nature and Seasons
Rainbow

Nature and Seasons
Scarf

Nature and Seasons
Snowflake

Nature and Seasons
Storm

Nature and Seasons
Sun

Nature and Seasons
Sunflower

Nature and Seasons
Tree

Nature and Seasons
Umbrella

Nature and Seasons
Wellies

Party
Balloon

Party
Cupcake

Cartoons - Silhouette

Party
Party Blower

Party
Party Hat

Party
Party Popper

Professions
Butcher

Professions
Doctor

Professions
Fire Officer

Professions
Mechanic

Professions
Paramedic

Professions
Plumber

Professions
Police Officer

Professions
Postman

Transport
Bus Front

Transport
Bus Side

Transport
Car 01

Transport
Car 02

Transport
Dump Truck

Transport
Dumpster

Transport
Forklift Truck

Transport
Helicopter

Transport
Jet

Transport
Motorcycle

Transport
Motorhome

Transport
Petrol Pump

Transport
Scooter

Transport
Ship

Cartoons - Silhouette

Transport
Taxi

Transport
Tractor

Transport
Train

Transport
Tram

Wedding
Bells

Wedding
Bouquet

Wedding
Cake

Wedding
Church

Wedding
Garter

Wedding
Horseshoe

Wedding
Just Married
Sign

Wedding
Limousine

Wedding
Top Hat

Zodiac Signs
Aquarius

Zodiac Signs
Aries

Zodiac Signs
Cancer

Zodiac Signs
Capricorn

Zodiac Signs
Gemini

Zodiac Signs
Leo

Zodiac Signs
Libra

Zodiac Signs
Pisces

Zodiac Signs
Sagittarius

Zodiac Signs
Scorpio

Zodiac Signs
Taurus

Zodiac Signs
Virgo

Connecting Symbols

Computers
Bridge

Computers
Camera

Computers
Cell Phone

Computers
Comm-link

Computers
Comm-link_2

Computers
CRT

Computers
CRT_2

Computers
Ethernet

Computers
Fax

Computers
Firewall

Computers
Hub

Computers
Modem

Computers
PC Unit

Computers
Photocopier

Computers
Printer

Computers
Projector

Computers
Router

Computers
Scanner

Computers
Screen

Computers
Switch

Computers
Telephone

Computers
TFT

Computers
User

Computers
Video Camera

Computers
Wireless Router

Computers
Wireless

Connecting Symbols - Electronics

Electronics

**Antennas and
Meters**
Amp Meter

**Antennas and
Meters**
Antenna A

**Antennas and
Meters**
Antenna B

**Antennas and
Meters**
Antenna Diple

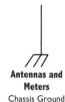

**Antennas and
Meters**
Chassis Ground

**Antennas and
Meters**
Current Source

**Antennas and
Meters**
Earth Ground

**Antennas and
Meters**
General Ground

**Antennas and
Meters**
Saw Wave
Source

**Antennas and
Meters**
Sine Wave
Source

**Antennas and
Meters**
Square Wave
Source

**Antennas and
Meters**
Volt Meter

**Antennas and
Meters**
Watt Meter

**Cells and
Connectors**
117v Female
Connector

**Cells and
Connectors**
117v Male
Chassis Mt

**Cells and
Connectors**
117v Male
Connector

**Cells and
Connectors**
234v Female
Connector

**Cells and
Connectors**
Circuit Breaker

**Cells and
Connectors**
Coaxial Plug
Male

**Cells and
Connectors**
Coaxial
Receptacle Fm

**Cells and
Connectors**
Crystal Quartz

**Cells and
Connectors**
Engaged
Contacts

**Cells and
Connectors**
Female Contact
Jack

Connecting Symbols - Electronics

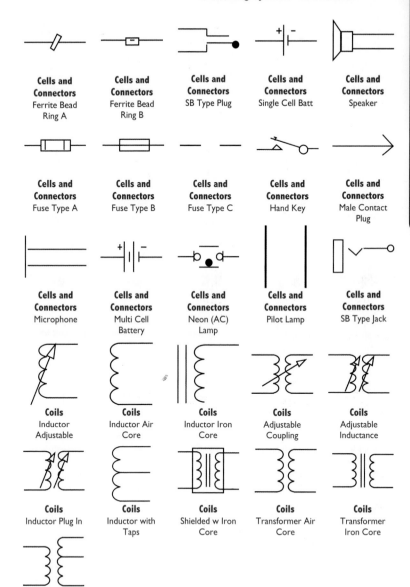

Cells and Connectors
Ferrite Bead Ring A

Cells and Connectors
Ferrite Bead Ring B

Cells and Connectors
SB Type Plug

Cells and Connectors
Single Cell Batt

Cells and Connectors
Speaker

Cells and Connectors
Fuse Type A

Cells and Connectors
Fuse Type B

Cells and Connectors
Fuse Type C

Cells and Connectors
Hand Key

Cells and Connectors
Male Contact Plug

Cells and Connectors
Microphone

Cells and Connectors
Multi Cell Battery

Cells and Connectors
Neon (AC) Lamp

Cells and Connectors
Pilot Lamp

Cells and Connectors
SB Type Jack

Coils
Inductor Adjustable

Coils
Inductor Air Core

Coils
Inductor Iron Core

Coils
Adjustable Coupling

Coils
Adjustable Inductance

Coils
Inductor Plug In

Coils
Inductor with Taps

Coils
Shielded w Iron Core

Coils
Transformer Air Core

Coils
Transformer Iron Core

Coils
Transformer with Link

Connecting Symbols - Electronics

Components and Logic Gates
Amplifier

Components and Logic Gates
Capacitor Electrolytic

Components and Logic Gates
Capacitor Feedthrough

Components and Logic Gates
Capacitor Fixed

Components and Logic Gates
Capacitor Split Stator

Components and Logic Gates
Capacitor Variable

Components and Logic Gates
Diode Capacitive

Components and Logic Gates
Diode Light Emitting

Components and Logic Gates
Diode Schottky

Components and Logic Gates
Diode Thyristor (SCR)

Components and Logic Gates
Diode Triac

Components and Logic Gates
Diode Tunnel

Components and Logic Gates
Diode Varactor

Components and Logic Gates
Diode Zener

Components and Logic Gates
Diode

Components and Logic Gates
Gate AND Inhibited

Components and Logic Gates
Gate AND

Components and Logic Gates
Gate NAND

Components and Logic Gates
Gate NOR

Components and Logic Gates
Gate OR Exclusive

Components and Logic Gates
Gate OR

Components and Logic Gates
Invertor

Components and Logic Gates
Resistor Adjustable

Components and Logic Gates
Resistor Fixed

Components and Logic Gates
Resistor Preset

Connecting Symbols - Electronics

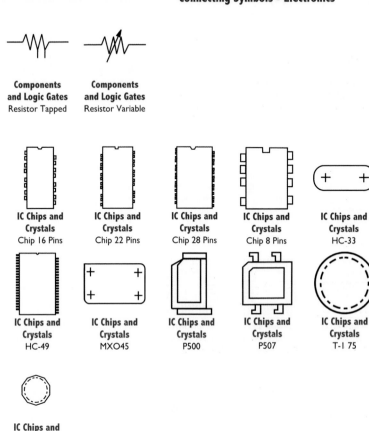

**Components
and Logic Gates**
Resistor Tapped

**Components
and Logic Gates**
Resistor Variable

**IC Chips and
Crystals**
Chip 16 Pins

**IC Chips and
Crystals**
Chip 22 Pins

**IC Chips and
Crystals**
Chip 28 Pins

**IC Chips and
Crystals**
Chip 8 Pins

**IC Chips and
Crystals**
HC-33

**IC Chips and
Crystals**
HC-49

**IC Chips and
Crystals**
MXO45

**IC Chips and
Crystals**
P500

**IC Chips and
Crystals**
P507

**IC Chips and
Crystals**
T-1 75

**IC Chips and
Crystals**
T-1

PCB Pads
DB 15
Connector

PCB Pads
DB 25
Connector

PCB Pads
DB 37
Connector

PCB Pads
DB 9 Connector

PCB Pads
Edge Card
Connector 25
Conductor

Connecting Symbols - Electronics

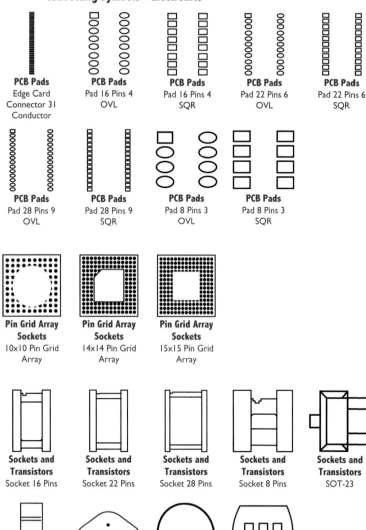

PCB Pads
Edge Card
Connector 31
Conductor

PCB Pads
Pad 16 Pins 4
OVL

PCB Pads
Pad 16 Pins 4
SQR

PCB Pads
Pad 22 Pins 6
OVL

PCB Pads
Pad 22 Pins 6
SQR

PCB Pads
Pad 28 Pins 9
OVL

PCB Pads
Pad 28 Pins 9
SQR

PCB Pads
Pad 8 Pins 3
OVL

PCB Pads
Pad 8 Pins 3
SQR

**Pin Grid Array
Sockets**
10x10 Pin Grid
Array

**Pin Grid Array
Sockets**
14x14 Pin Grid
Array

**Pin Grid Array
Sockets**
15x15 Pin Grid
Array

**Sockets and
Transistors**
Socket 16 Pins

**Sockets and
Transistors**
Socket 22 Pins

**Sockets and
Transistors**
Socket 28 Pins

**Sockets and
Transistors**
Socket 8 Pins

**Sockets and
Transistors**
SOT-23

**Sockets and
Transistors**
TO-220

**Sockets and
Transistors**
TO-3

**Sockets and
Transistors**
TO-39

**Sockets and
Transistors**
TO-92

Connecting Symbols - Electronics

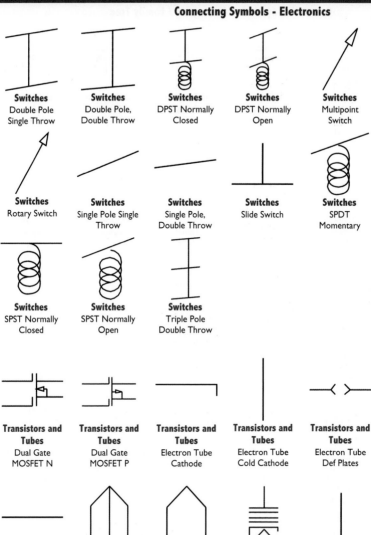

Switches
Double Pole
Single Throw

Switches
Double Pole,
Double Throw

Switches
DPST Normally
Closed

Switches
DPST Normally
Open

Switches
Multipoint
Switch

Switches
Rotary Switch

Switches
Single Pole Single
Throw

Switches
Single Pole,
Double Throw

Switches
Slide Switch

Switches
SPDT
Momentary

Switches
SPST Normally
Closed

Switches
SPST Normally
Open

Switches
Triple Pole
Double Throw

**Transistors and
Tubes**
Dual Gate
MOSFET N

**Transistors and
Tubes**
Dual Gate
MOSFET P

**Transistors and
Tubes**
Electron Tube
Cathode

**Transistors and
Tubes**
Electron Tube
Cold Cathode

**Transistors and
Tubes**
Electron Tube
Def Plates

**Transistors and
Tubes**
Electron Tube
Grid

**Transistors and
Tubes**
Electron Tube
Heater A

**Transistors and
Tubes**
Electron Tube
Heater B

**Transistors and
Tubes**
Electron Tube
Pentode

**Transistors and
Tubes**
Electron Tube
Plate

Connecting Symbols - Electronics / Family Tree

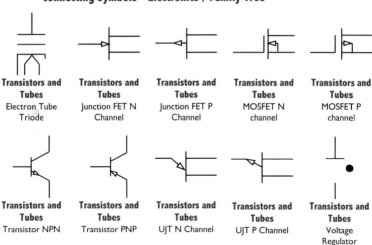

Transistors and Tubes
Electron Tube Triode

Transistors and Tubes
Junction FET N Channel

Transistors and Tubes
Junction FET P Channel

Transistors and Tubes
MOSFET N channel

Transistors and Tubes
MOSFET P channel

Transistors and Tubes
Transistor NPN

Transistors and Tubes
Transistor PNP

Transistors and Tubes
UJT N Channel

Transistors and Tubes
UJT P Channel

Transistors and Tubes
Voltage Regulator

Family Tree

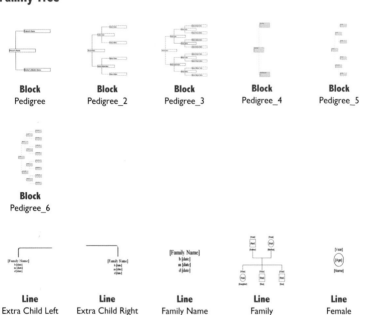

Block
Pedigree

Block
Pedigree_2

Block
Pedigree_3

Block
Pedigree_4

Block
Pedigree_5

Block
Pedigree_6

Line
Extra Child Left

Line
Extra Child Right

Line
Family Name

Line
Family

Line
Female

Connecting Symbols - Family Tree

Line
Male

Line
Marriage

Line
Pedigree_7

Line
Single Child

Line
Three Children

Line
Two Children

Photographic
Frame and
Nameplate

Photographic
Frame and
Nameplate_2

Photographic
Single Frame

Photographic
Single Frame_2

Photographic
Single Photo
Frame

Photographic
Single Photo
Frame_2

Photographic
Wooden Frame

Photographic
Wooden
Frame_2

Photographic
Wooden
Frame_3

Photographic
Wooden
Frame_4

Photographic
Wooden
Frame_5

Connecting Symbols - FlowCharts

FlowCharts

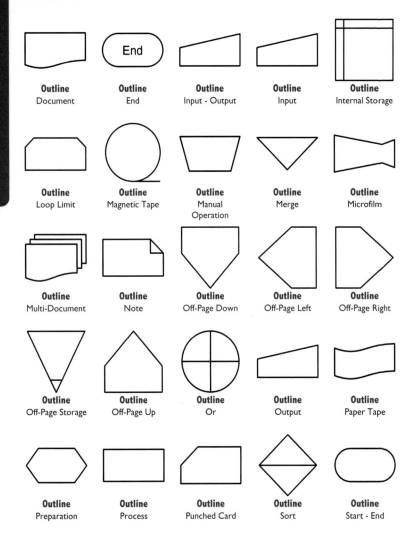

Outline
Document

Outline
End

Outline
Input - Output

Outline
Input

Outline
Internal Storage

Outline
Loop Limit

Outline
Magnetic Tape

Outline
Manual Operation

Outline
Merge

Outline
Microfilm

Outline
Multi-Document

Outline
Note

Outline
Off-Page Down

Outline
Off-Page Left

Outline
Off-Page Right

Outline
Off-Page Storage

Outline
Off-Page Up

Outline
Or

Outline
Output

Outline
Paper Tape

Outline
Preparation

Outline
Process

Outline
Punched Card

Outline
Sort

Outline
Start - End

Connecting Symbols - FlowCharts

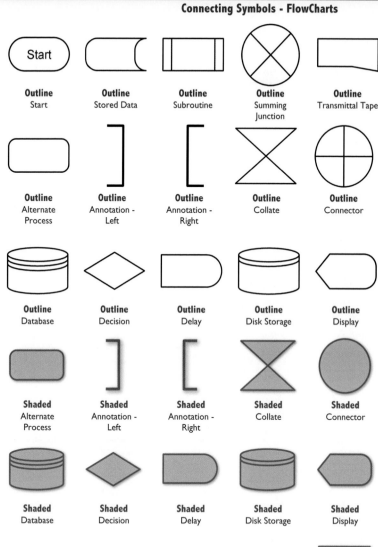

Outline
Start

Outline
Stored Data

Outline
Subroutine

Outline
Summing
Junction

Outline
Transmittal Tape

Outline
Alternate
Process

Outline
Annotation -
Left

Outline
Annotation -
Right

Outline
Collate

Outline
Connector

Outline
Database

Outline
Decision

Outline
Delay

Outline
Disk Storage

Outline
Display

Shaded
Alternate
Process

Shaded
Annotation -
Left

Shaded
Annotation -
Right

Shaded
Collate

Shaded
Connector

Shaded
Database

Shaded
Decision

Shaded
Delay

Shaded
Disk Storage

Shaded
Display

Shaded
Document

Shaded
End

Shaded
Input - Output

Shaded
Input

Shaded
Internal Storage

Connecting Symbols - FlowCharts

Shaded
Loop Limit

Shaded
Magnetic Tape

Shaded
Manual
Operation

Shaded
Merge

Shaded
Microfilm

Shaded
Multi-Document

Shaded
Note

Shaded
Off-Page Down

Shaded
Off-Page Left

Shaded
Off-Page Right

Shaded
Off-Page Storage

Shaded
Off-Page Up

Shaded
Or

Shaded
Output

Shaded
Paper Tape

Shaded
Preparation

Shaded
Process

Shaded
Punched Card

Shaded
Sort

Shaded
Start - End

Shaded
Start

Shaded
Stored Data

Shaded
Subroutine

Shaded
Summing
Junction

Shaded
Transmittal Tape

Connecting Symbols - Orginizational Chart

Orginizational Chart

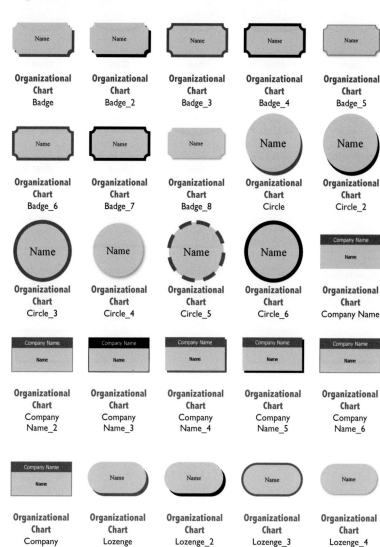

Organizational Chart Badge

Organizational Chart Badge_2

Organizational Chart Badge_3

Organizational Chart Badge_4

Organizational Chart Badge_5

Organizational Chart Badge_6

Organizational Chart Badge_7

Organizational Chart Badge_8

Organizational Chart Circle

Organizational Chart Circle_2

Organizational Chart Circle_3

Organizational Chart Circle_4

Organizational Chart Circle_5

Organizational Chart Circle_6

Organizational Chart Company Name

Organizational Chart Company Name_2

Organizational Chart Company Name_3

Organizational Chart Company Name_4

Organizational Chart Company Name_5

Organizational Chart Company Name_6

Organizational Chart Company Name_7

Organizational Chart Lozenge

Organizational Chart Lozenge_2

Organizational Chart Lozenge_3

Organizational Chart Lozenge_4

Connecting Symbols - Orginizational Chart

**Organizational
Chart**
Lozenge_5

**Organizational
Chart**
Lozenge_6

**Organizational
Chart**
Oval

**Organizational
Chart**
Oval_2

**Organizational
Chart**
Oval_3

**Organizational
Chart**
Oval_4

**Organizational
Chart**
Oval_5

**Organizational
Chart**
Oval_6

**Organizational
Chart**
Rectangle_I

**Organizational
Chart**
Rectangle_2

**Organizational
Chart**
Rectangle_3

**Organizational
Chart**
Rectangle_4

**Organizational
Chart**
Rectangle_5

**Organizational
Chart**
Rectangle_6

**Organizational
Chart**
Rounded
Rectangle

**Organizational
Chart**
Rounded
Rectangle_2

**Organizational
Chart**
Rounded
Rectangle_3

**Organizational
Chart**
Rounded
Rectangle_4

**Organizational
Chart**
Rounded
Rectangle_5

**Organizational
Chart**
Rounded
Rectangle_6

Connecting Symbols - Web Diagram

Web Diagram

Web Diagram
Audio File

Web Diagram
Audio

Web Diagram
Blog

Web Diagram
Blog_2

Web Diagram
Client Side
Script

Web Diagram
Cloud

Web Diagram
Database

Web Diagram
Download

Web Diagram
Download_2

Web Diagram
Download_3

Web Diagram
File

Web Diagram
Form

Web Diagram
FTP

Web Diagram
Gopher

Web Diagram
Hard Copy

Web Diagram
Home Page

Web Diagram
Home

Web Diagram
HTML Page

Web Diagram
Internet
Terminal

Web Diagram
Java Page

Web Diagram
Jump Page

Web Diagram
Mail To

Web Diagram
Movie

Web Diagram
News Group

Web Diagram
News Group_2

Connecting Symbols - Web Diagram

Web Diagram
News

Web Diagram
News_2

Web Diagram
Non-Secure
Page

Web Diagram
Non-Secure

Web Diagram
Off Site Link

Web Diagram
Page

Web Diagram
Page_2

Web Diagram
Page_3

Web Diagram
Plug-in

Web Diagram
R-Login

Web Diagram
Search

Web Diagram
Search_2

Web Diagram
Secure Page

Web Diagram
Secure

Web Diagram
Server Side
Script

Web Diagram
Style Sheet

Web Diagram
Telnet

Web Diagram
Terminal

Web Diagram
Web Page

Web Diagram
Web Services

Web Diagram
www

Web Diagram
XML Page

Curriculum

Design & Technology

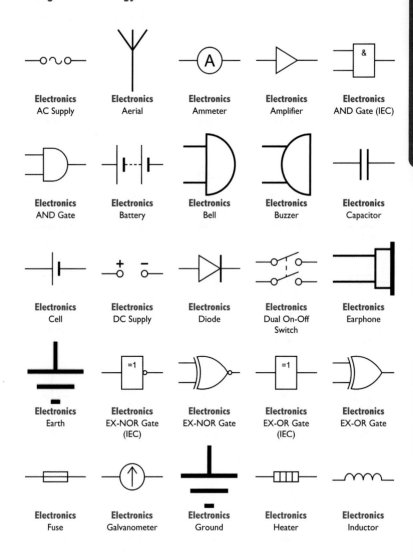

Electronics
AC Supply

Electronics
Aerial

Electronics
Ammeter

Electronics
Amplifier

Electronics
AND Gate (IEC)

Electronics
AND Gate

Electronics
Battery

Electronics
Bell

Electronics
Buzzer

Electronics
Capacitor

Electronics
Cell

Electronics
DC Supply

Electronics
Diode

Electronics
Dual On-Off
Switch

Electronics
Earphone

Electronics
Earth

Electronics
EX-NOR Gate
(IEC)

Electronics
EX-NOR Gate

Electronics
EX-OR Gate
(IEC)

Electronics
EX-OR Gate

Electronics
Fuse

Electronics
Galvanometer

Electronics
Ground

Electronics
Heater

Electronics
Inductor

Curriculum - Design & Technology

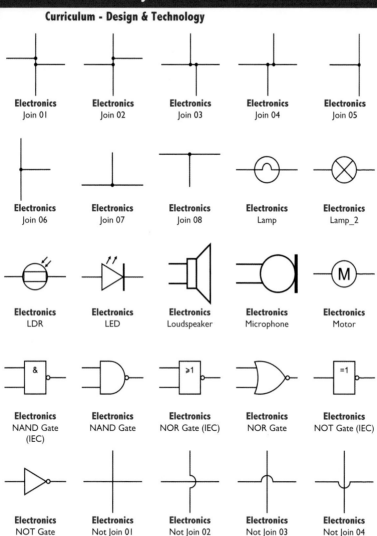

Electronics Join 01	**Electronics** Join 02	**Electronics** Join 03	**Electronics** Join 04	**Electronics** Join 05
Electronics Join 06	**Electronics** Join 07	**Electronics** Join 08	**Electronics** Lamp	**Electronics** Lamp_2
Electronics LDR	**Electronics** LED	**Electronics** Loudspeaker	**Electronics** Microphone	**Electronics** Motor
Electronics NAND Gate (IEC)	**Electronics** NAND Gate	**Electronics** NOR Gate (IEC)	**Electronics** NOR Gate	**Electronics** NOT Gate (IEC)
Electronics NOT Gate	**Electronics** Not Join 01	**Electronics** Not Join 02	**Electronics** Not Join 03	**Electronics** Not Join 04
Electronics Not Join 05	**Electronics** Ohmmeter	**Electronics** On-Off Switch	**Electronics** OR Gate (IEC)	**Electronics** OR Gate

Curriculum - Design & Technology

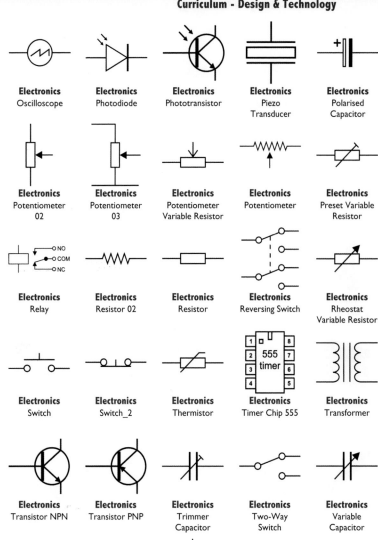

Electronics
Oscilloscope

Electronics
Photodiode

Electronics
Phototransistor

Electronics
Piezo
Transducer

Electronics
Polarised
Capacitor

Electronics
Potentiometer
02

Electronics
Potentiometer
03

Electronics
Potentiometer
Variable Resistor

Electronics
Potentiometer

Electronics
Preset Variable
Resistor

Electronics
Relay

Electronics
Resistor 02

Electronics
Resistor

Electronics
Reversing Switch

Electronics
Rheostat
Variable Resistor

Electronics
Switch

Electronics
Switch_2

Electronics
Thermistor

Electronics
Timer Chip 555

Electronics
Transformer

Electronics
Transistor NPN

Electronics
Transistor PNP

Electronics
Trimmer
Capacitor

Electronics
Two-Way
Switch

Electronics
Variable
Capacitor

Electronics
Variable Resistor
02

Electronics
Variable Resistor
03

Electronics
Variable Resistor

Electronics
Voltmeter

Electronics
Zener Diode

Curriculum - Design & Technology

Food
Cake Knife

Food
Chef Hat

Food
Food Processor

Food
Handheld Mixer

Food
Knife

Food
Rolling Pin

Food
Salt & Pepper

Food
Scales

Food
Spoon

Food
Toaster

Food
Wooden Spoons

General
Cutting Board

General
Eraser

General
Hammer

General
Knife

General
Paintbrush

General
Pencil

General
Ruler

General
Saw

General
Scissors

General
Scraper

General
Stationery
Stencil

General
Tape

Geography

Flags
Austria

Flags
Belgium

Flags
Cyprus

Flags
Czech Republic

Flags
Denmark

Flags
England

Flags
Estonia

Flags
European Union

Flags
Finland

Flags
France

Flags
Germany

Flags
Great Britain

Flags
Greece

Flags
Hungary

Flags
Ireland

Flags
Italy

Flags
Latvia

Flags
Lithuania

Flags
Luxembourg

Flags
Malta

Flags
Netherlands

Flags
Poland

Flags
Portugal

Flags
Scotland

Flags
Slovakia

Flags
Slovenia

Flags
Spain

Flags
Sweden

Flags
United States of
America

Flags
Wales

Curriculum - Geography

Weather
Bright Slight
Clouds

Weather
Clouds some
Sunshine

Weather
Cloudy - Night

Weather
Cloudy

Weather
Dark Clouds
with Rain - Night

Weather
Dark Clouds
with Rain

Weather
Dark Clouds

Weather
Fog - Night

Weather
Hazy

Weather
Heavy Rain

Weather
Icy Blizzard -
Night

Weather
Icy Blizzard

Weather
Lightning Storm
- Night

Weather
Lightning Storm

Weather
Mild Sunshine

Weather
Showers - Night

Weather
Showers

Weather
Snow

Weather
Sunny Showers

Weather
Very Sunny

Weather
Snow - Night

Curriculum - Maths / Science - Biology

Maths

Maths - Colour
Abacus 01

Maths - Colour
Abacus 02

Maths - Colour
pi

Maths - Colour
Protractor

Maths - Colour
Ruler

Maths - Colour
Set Square 01

Maths - Colour
Set Square 02

Maths - Outline
Abacus 01

Maths - Outline
Abacus 02

Maths - Outline
pi

Maths - Outline
Protractor

Maths - Outline
Ruler

Maths - Outline
Set Square 01

Maths - Outline
Set Square 02

Science - Biology

**Diagrams -
Colour**
Dna

**Diagrams -
Colour**
Heart

**Diagrams -
Colour**
Intestines

**Diagrams -
Colour**
Lungs

**Diagrams -
Colour**
Microscope

Curriculum - Science - Biology / Chemistry

**Diagrams -
Colour**
Retina

**Diagrams -
Silhouette**
Dna

**Diagrams -
Silhouette**
Heart

**Diagrams -
Silhouette**
Intestines

**Diagrams -
Silhouette**
Lungs

**Diagrams -
Silhouette**
Microscope

**Diagrams -
Silhouette**
Retina

**Diagrams -
Silhouette**
Synovial Joint

Science - Chemistry

**Laboratory
Equipment**
Beaker

**Laboratory
Equipment**
Boiling Tube

**Laboratory
Equipment**
Bung

**Laboratory
Equipment**
Bunsen Burner
and Tripod

**Laboratory
Equipment**
Bunsen Burner

**Laboratory
Equipment**
Condenser

**Laboratory
Equipment**
Conical Flask

**Laboratory
Equipment**
Crucible

**Laboratory
Equipment**
Drying Tube

**Laboratory
Equipment**
Erlenmeyer Flask

Curriculum - Science - Chemistry

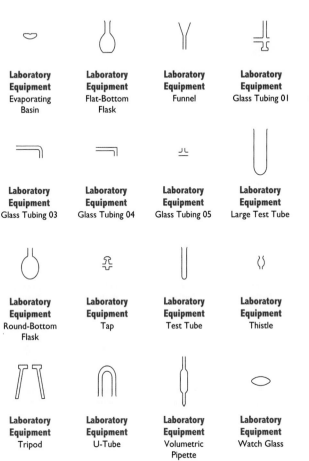

Laboratory Equipment
Evaporating Basin

Laboratory Equipment
Flat-Bottom Flask

Laboratory Equipment
Funnel

Laboratory Equipment
Glass Tubing 01

Laboratory Equipment
Glass Tubing 02

Laboratory Equipment
Glass Tubing 03

Laboratory Equipment
Glass Tubing 04

Laboratory Equipment
Glass Tubing 05

Laboratory Equipment
Large Test Tube

Laboratory Equipment
Measuring Cylinder

Laboratory Equipment
Round-Bottom Flask

Laboratory Equipment
Tap

Laboratory Equipment
Test Tube

Laboratory Equipment
Thistle

Laboratory Equipment
Three Way Adapter

Laboratory Equipment
Tripod

Laboratory Equipment
U-Tube

Laboratory Equipment
Volumetric Pipette

Laboratory Equipment
Watch Glass

Symbols - Colour
Beaker

Symbols - Colour
Benzene

Symbols - Colour
Burette

Symbols - Colour
Clamp

Symbols - Colour
Conical Flask

Curriculum - Science - Chemistry

Symbols - Colour
Dropper

Symbols - Colour
Evaporating Dish

Symbols - Colour
Graduated Cylinder

Symbols - Colour
Pipette

Symbols - Colour
Spatula

Symbols - Colour
Test Tube

Symbols - Colour
Tripod

Symbols - Outline
Beaker

Symbols - Outline
Bunsen Burner

Symbols - Outline
Burette

Symbols - Outline
Conical Flask

Symbols - Outline
Dropper

Symbols - Outline
Graduated Cylinder

Symbols - Outline
Pipette

Symbols - Outline
Test Tube 01

Symbols - Outline
Test Tube 02

Symbols - Outline
Test Tube 03

Symbols - Outline
Tripod

Curriculum - Science - Chemistry / Physics

**Symbols -
Silhouette**
Beaker

**Symbols -
Silhouette**
Bunsen Burner

**Symbols -
Silhouette**
Burette

**Symbols -
Silhouette**
Clamp

**Symbols -
Silhouette**
Conical Flask

**Symbols -
Silhouette**
Dropper

**Symbols -
Silhouette**
Graduated
Cylinder

**Symbols -
Silhouette**
Pipette

**Symbols -
Silhouette**
Spatula

**Symbols -
Silhouette**
Test Tube

**Symbols -
Silhouette**
Tripod

Science - Physics

**Symbols -
Colour**
Atomic
Structure

**Symbols -
Colour**
Blackboard
Formula

**Symbols -
Colour**
Magnet

**Symbols -
Colour**
Newton Cradle

**Symbols -
Colour**
Oscilloscope

**Symbols -
Colour**
Telescope

Curriculum - Science - Physics / Sports

Symbols - Silhouette
Atomic Structure

Symbols - Silhouette
Blackboard Formula

Symbols - Silhouette
Magnet

Symbols - Silhouette
Oscilloscope

Sports

Game Templates
Baseball Pitch

Game Templates
Basketball Court

Game Templates
Chess Board

Game Templates
Cricket Pitch

Game Templates
Football Pitch

Game Templates
Hockey Pitch

Game Templates
Rugby Pitch

Game Templates
Snooker Table

Game Templates
Tennis Clay Court

Game Templates
Tennis Grass Court

Sports Equipment
Bench

Sports Equipment
Dumbbell

Sports Equipment
Skip Rope

Sports Equipment
Stop Watch

Sports Equipment
Trampoline

Sports Equipment
Treadmill

Sports Equipment
Weights

Curriculum - Sports

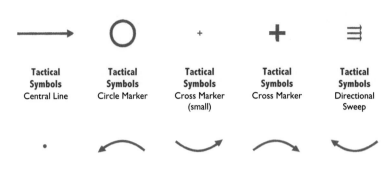

**Tactical
Symbols**
Central Line

**Tactical
Symbols**
Circle Marker

**Tactical
Symbols**
Cross Marker
(small)

**Tactical
Symbols**
Cross Marker

**Tactical
Symbols**
Directional
Sweep

**Tactical
Symbols**
Player Marker

**Tactical
Symbols**
Wing Arrow
(down left)

**Tactical
Symbols**
Wing Arrow
(down right)

**Tactical
Symbols**
Wing Arrow (up
left)

**Tactical
Symbols**
Wing Arrow (up
right)

**Tactical
Symbols**
X Marker (small)

**Tactical
Symbols**
X Marker

Layout Symbols - Garden

Layout Symbols

Garden

Bedding
Bedding I blue

Bedding
Bedding I mauve

Bedding
Bedding I pink

Bedding
Bedding I red

Bedding
Bedding I white

Bedding
Bedding I yellow

Bedding
Bedding 2
bronze

Bedding
Bedding 2 cool
green

Bedding
Bedding 2 dark
green

Bedding
Bedding 3
bronze

Bedding
Bedding 3 cool
green

Bedding
Bedding 3 dark
green

**Buildings and
Fixtures**
Apex roof shed

**Buildings and
Fixtures**
Arbour

**Buildings and
Fixtures**
Brick wall
section

**Buildings and
Fixtures**
Brick wall with
return

**Buildings and
Fixtures**
Bridge I

Layout Symbols - Garden

Buildings and Fixtures
Bridge 2

Buildings and Fixtures
Cold frame

Buildings and Fixtures
Fence panel and post - blue

Buildings and Fixtures
Fence panel and post - brown

Buildings and Fixtures
Fence panel and post - cedar

Buildings and Fixtures
Fence panel and post - green

Buildings and Fixtures
Medium greenhouse

Buildings and Fixtures
Octagon summerhouse

Buildings and Fixtures
Pent roof shed

Buildings and Fixtures
Pergola section - blue

Buildings and Fixtures
Pergola section - brown

Buildings and Fixtures
Pergola section - cedar

Buildings and Fixtures
Pergola section - green

Buildings and Fixtures
Sentry box store

Buildings and Fixtures
Small greenhouse

Buildings and Fixtures
Summerhouse

Layout Symbols - Garden

Containers
Container I
black

Containers
Container I blue

Containers
Container I
brown

Containers
Container I
cream

Containers
Container I grey

Containers
Container I
terracotta

Containers
Container 2
black

Containers
Container 2 blue

Containers
Container 2
brown

Containers
Container 2
cream

Containers
Container 2 grey

Containers
Container 2
terracotta

Containers
Container 3
black

Containers
Container 3 blue

Containers
Container 3
brown

Containers
Container 3
cream

Containers
Container 3 grey

Containers
Container 3
terracotta

Containers
Container 4
black

Containers
Container 4 blue

Layout Symbols - Garden

Containers
Container 4
brown

Containers
Container 4
cream

Containers
Container 4 grey

Containers
Container 4
terracotta

Furniture
Barbecue

Furniture
Blue patio chair

Furniture
Blue patio table
1

Furniture
Blue patio table
2

Furniture
Blue patio table
3

Furniture
Blue patio table
4

Furniture
Blue patio
umbrella

Furniture
Garden seat

Furniture
Gnome

Furniture
Green patio
umbrella

Furniture
Kid's slide

Furniture
Natural patio
chair

Furniture
Natural patio
table 1

Furniture
Natural patio
table 2

Furniture
Natural patio
table 3

Layout Symbols - Garden

Furniture
Natural patio
table 4

Furniture
Sandpit

Furniture
Teak patio chair

Furniture
Teak patio table
1

Furniture
Teak patio table
2

Furniture
Teak patio table
3

Furniture
Teak patio table
4

Furniture
Terrace seating
area - blue

Furniture
Terrace seating
area - natural

Furniture
Terrace seating
area - teak

Furniture
Trampoline

Furniture
Yellow patio
umbrella

**Hedges, Shrubs
and Trees**
Hedge cool
green

**Hedges, Shrubs
and Trees**
Hedge dark
green

**Hedges, Shrubs
and Trees**
Large tree

**Hedges, Shrubs
and Trees**
Leylandii hedge

**Hedges, Shrubs
and Trees**
Medium tree

Layout Symbols - Garden

Hedges, Shrubs and Trees
Shrub 1 cool green

Hedges, Shrubs and Trees
Shrub 1 evergreen

Hedges, Shrubs and Trees
Shrub 10 bronze

Hedges, Shrubs and Trees
Shrub 10 cool green

Hedges, Shrubs and Trees
Shrub 10 dark green

Hedges, Shrubs and Trees
Shrub 2 bronze

Hedges, Shrubs and Trees
Shrub 2 cool green

Hedges, Shrubs and Trees
Shrub 2 dark green

Hedges, Shrubs and Trees
Shrub 3 bronze

Hedges, Shrubs and Trees
Shrub 3 cool green

Hedges, Shrubs and Trees
Shrub 3 dark green

Hedges, Shrubs and Trees
Shrub 4 bronze

Hedges, Shrubs and Trees
Shrub 4 cool green

Hedges, Shrubs and Trees
Shrub 4 dark green

Hedges, Shrubs and Trees
Shrub 5 bronze

Hedges, Shrubs and Trees
Shrub 5 cool green

Hedges, Shrubs and Trees
Shrub 5 dark green

Hedges, Shrubs and Trees
Shrub 6 dark green

Hedges, Shrubs and Trees
Shrub 6 red-green

Hedges, Shrubs and Trees
Shrub 6 silver grey

Layout Symbols - Garden

Hedges, Shrubs and Trees
Shrub 9 pale green

Hedges, Shrubs and Trees
Small tree

Hedges, Shrubs and Trees
Shrub 7 cool green

Hedges, Shrubs and Trees
Shrub 7 dark green

Hedges, Shrubs and Trees
Shrub 7 yellow-green

Hedges, Shrubs and Trees
Shrub 8 blue

Hedges, Shrubs and Trees
Shrub 8 mauve

Hedges, Shrubs and Trees
Shrub 8 pink

Hedges, Shrubs and Trees
Shrub 8 red

Hedges, Shrubs and Trees
Shrub 8 white

Hedges, Shrubs and Trees
Shrub 8 yellow

Hedges, Shrubs and Trees
Shrub 9 bronze

Hedges, Shrubs and Trees
Shrub 9 dark green

Surfaces and Features
Bark chip area

Surfaces and Features
Bedding area 1

Surfaces and Features
Bedding area 2

Surfaces and Features
Bedding area 3

Surfaces and Features
Bedding area 4

Layout Symbols - Garden

Surfaces and Features
Bedding area 5

Surfaces and Features
Bedding area 6

Surfaces and Features
Bedding area 7

Surfaces and Features
Border area 1

Surfaces and Features
Border area 2

Surfaces and Features
Border area 3

Surfaces and Features
Border area 4

Surfaces and Features
Coir matting section

Surfaces and Features
Curved path section 1

Surfaces and Features
Curved path section 2

Surfaces and Features
Curved path section 3

Surfaces and Features
Decking section blue

Surfaces and Features
Decking section natural

Surfaces and Features
Gravel area

Surfaces and Features
Large pond 1

Surfaces and Features
Large pond 2

Surfaces and Features
Lawn 1

Surfaces and Features
Lawn 10

Surfaces and Features
Lawn 2

Surfaces and Features
Lawn 3

Layout Symbols - Garden

Surfaces and Features
Lawn 4

Surfaces and Features
Lawn 5

Surfaces and Features
Lawn 6

Surfaces and Features
Lawn 7

Surfaces and Features
Lawn 8

Surfaces and Features
Lawn 9

Surfaces and Features
Patio edging 1

Surfaces and Features
Patio edging 2

Surfaces and Features
Patio surface 1

Surfaces and Features
Patio surface 2

Surfaces and Features
Patio surface 3

Surfaces and Features
Patio surface 4

Surfaces and Features
Patio surface 5

Surfaces and Features
Patio surface 6

Surfaces and Features
Pebble area

Surfaces and Features
Rockery corner

Surfaces and Features
Rockery

Surfaces and Features
Small pond 1

Surfaces and Features
Small pond 2

Surfaces and Features
Stone chippings area 1

Layout Symbols - Garden / Home

Surfaces and Features
Stone chippings area 2

Surfaces and Features
Stone chippings area 3

Surfaces and Features
Straight path section 1

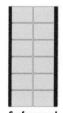

Surfaces and Features
Straight path section 2

Surfaces and Features
Straight path section 3

Surfaces and Features
Stream 1

Surfaces and Features
Stream 2

Surfaces and Features
White sand area 2

Home

Beds
Bunk bed

Beds
Crib

Beds
Double bed with drawers

Beds
Double bed

Beds
Futon bed as seat

Layout Symbols - Home

Beds
Futon bed

Beds
King size bed

Beds
Single bed

Beds
Super King size
bed

Cabinets
Corner cabinet

Cabinets
Display cabinet

Cabinets
Long cabinet

Cabinets
Long Display
cabinet

Cabinets
Small cabinet

Cabinets
Wide cabinet

**Kitchen
Cabinets**
12inch deep
narrow wall
cupboard

**Kitchen
Cabinets**
12inch deep wall
cabinet

**Kitchen
Cabinets**
12inch deep wall
LHS corner
cupboard

**Kitchen
Cabinets**
12inch deep wall
RHS corner
cupboard

**Kitchen
Cabinets**
20inch deep LHS
wall corner
cabinet

**Kitchen
Cabinets**
20inch deep
narrow wall
cabinet

**Kitchen
Cabinets**
20inch deep RHS
wall corner
cabinet

**Kitchen
Cabinets**
20inch deep wall
cabinet

Layout Symbols - Home

Kitchen Cabinets
24inch deep floor cabinet

Kitchen Cabinets
24inch deep floor LHS corner cabinet

Kitchen Cabinets
24inch deep floor RHS corner cabinet

Kitchen Cabinets
24inch deep narrow floor cabinet

Kitchen Cabinets
4 foot length worktop 01

Kitchen Cabinets
4 foot length worktop 02

Kitchen Cabinets
4 foot length worktop 03

Kitchen Cabinets
Extractor hood 01

Kitchen Cabinets
Extractor hood 02

Kitchen Cabinets
Extractor hood 03

Leisure
Baby grand piano

Leisure
Billiards table

Leisure
Grand piano

Leisure
Micro HiFi system

Leisure
Midi HiFi system

Leisure
Music keyboard

Leisure
Portable TV

Leisure
Record turntable

Leisure
Standard HiFi system

Leisure
Standard TV

Layout Symbols - Home

Leisure
Table tennis table

Leisure
Upright piano

Leisure
VCR-DVD player

Leisure
Widescreen TV

Lighting
Ceiling lamp

Lighting
Double spotlight

Lighting
Floor lamp with spots

Lighting
Floor lamp

Lighting
Low voltage spotlight

Lighting
Low voltage track

Lighting
Pendant light

Lighting
Single spotlight

Lighting
Uplighter

Lighting
Wall lamp

Major Appliances
Chest freezer

Major Appliances
Cooker hood-extractor

Major Appliances
Cooker

Major Appliances
Range oven

Major Appliances
Two-zone hob

Layout Symbols - Home

**Major
Appliances**
Dishwasher

**Major
Appliances**
Five-zone hob

**Major
Appliances**
Four-zone hob

**Major
Appliances**
Microwave

**Major
Appliances**
Mini fridge

**Major
Appliances**
Upright fridge-
freezer

**Major
Appliances**
Washer or dryer

**Plumbing
Fixtures**
Belfast sink

**Plumbing
Fixtures**
Bidet

**Plumbing
Fixtures**
Corner bathtub

**Plumbing
Fixtures**
Corner shower
1

**Plumbing
Fixtures**
Corner shower
2

**Plumbing
Fixtures**
Corner sink

**Plumbing
Fixtures**
Double Belfast
sink

**Plumbing
Fixtures**
Double drainer

**Plumbing
Fixtures**
Double sink with
drainer

**Plumbing
Fixtures**
Double sink

Layout Symbols - Home

**Plumbing
Fixtures**
Mixer taps

**Plumbing
Fixtures**
Oval bathtub

**Plumbing
Fixtures**
Round HotTub

**Plumbing
Fixtures**
Shower cubicle

**Plumbing
Fixtures**
Shower head
unit front-on

**Plumbing
Fixtures**
Shower head
unit

**Plumbing
Fixtures**
Sink mixer taps

**Plumbing
Fixtures**
Sink with left
drainer

**Plumbing
Fixtures**
Sink with right
drainer

**Plumbing
Fixtures**
Small bathtub

**Plumbing
Fixtures**
Spacesaver sink

**Plumbing
Fixtures**
Square HotTub

**Plumbing
Fixtures**
Standard bathtub

**Plumbing
Fixtures**
Standard
washbasin

**Plumbing
Fixtures**
Toilet with
cistern

**Plumbing
Fixtures**
Toilet

**Plumbing
Fixtures**
Victorian
bathtub

**Plumbing
Fixtures**
Victorian
washbasin

**Plumbing
Fixtures**
Walk-in shower

Layout Symbols - Home

Seating
Armchair

Seating
Carver chair

Seating
DeLuxe recliner

Seating
Dining chair

Seating
Futon bed as
seat

Seating
Left corner unit

Seating
Modular seating

Seating
Modular table

Seating
Recliner

Seating
Right corner unit

Seating
Settle

Seating
Three-seater
sofa

Seating
Tub armchair

Seating
Two-seater sofa

Seating
Centre unit

Tables
4 place table

Tables
Oblong 6 place
table

Tables
Oblong 8 place
table

Tables
Oblong coffee
table

Tables
Oval 4 place
table

Layout Symbols - Home

Tables
Oval 6 place
table

Tables
Oval 8 place
table

Tables
Oval coffee table

Tables
Round 4 place
table

Tables
Round 6 place
table

Tables
Round 8 place
table

Tables
Round coffee
table

**Walls, Doors
and Windows**
12 foot wall

**Walls, Doors
and Windows**
Bay window

**Walls, Doors
and Windows**
Double doors

**Walls, Doors
and Windows**
Double Floor
Stairs

**Walls, Doors
and Windows**
Double window

**Walls, Doors
and Windows**
Single window

**Walls, Doors
and Windows**
Spiral Staircase

**Walls, Doors
and Windows**
Stairs

**Walls, Doors
and Windows**
Standard door -
left hand

**Walls, Doors
and Windows**
Standard door -
right hand

ShapeArt

Badges
Badge 01

Badges
Badge 02

Badges
Badge 03

Badges
Badge 04

Badges
Badge 05

Badges
Badge 06

Badges
Badge 07

Badges
Badge 08

Badges
Badge 09

Badges
Badge 10

Banners
Banner 01

Banners
Banner 02

Banners
Banner 03

Banners
Banner 04

Banners
Banner 05

Banners
Banner 06

Banners
Banner 07

Banners
Banner 08

Banners
Banner 09

Banners
Banner 10

**Embossed
Shapes**
Arrow 01

**Embossed
Shapes**
Arrow 02

**Embossed
Shapes**
Circle

**Embossed
Shapes**
Drop

**Embossed
Shapes**
Half Moon

ShapeArt

**Embossed
Shapes**
Heart

**Embossed
Shapes**
Semi Circle

**Embossed
Shapes**
Speech Bubble

**Embossed
Shapes**
Splat

**Embossed
Shapes**
Square

**Embossed
Shapes**
Star

**Embossed
Shapes**
Triangle

Gel Shapes
Arrow

Gel Shapes
Ball

Gel Shapes
Button

Gel Shapes
Diamond

Gel Shapes
Droplet

Gel Shapes
Heart

Gel Shapes
Pill

Gel Shapes
Ring

Gel Shapes
Shield

Gel Shapes
Star

Gel Shapes
Tube

Shields
Shield 01

Shields
Shield 02

Shields
Shield 03

Shields
Shield 04

Shields
Shield 05

Shields
Shield 06

Shields
Shield 07

Shields
Shield 08

Shields
Shield 09

Shields
Shield 10

Smilies
Angry

Smilies
Cheeky

Smilies
Cool

Smilies
Crying

Smilies
Duh

Smilies
Grin

Smilies
Rich

Smilies
Romantic

Smilies
Sleepy

Smilies
Surprise

Splats
Scribble 01

Splats
Scribble 02

Splats
Scribble 03

Splats
Scribble 04

Splats
Scribble 05

ShapeArt

Splats
Splodge 01

Splats
Splodge 02

Splats
Splodge 03

Splats
Splodge 04

Splats
Splodge 05

Splats
Splodge 06

Splats
Splat 01

Splats
Splat 02

Splats
Splat 03

Splats
Splat 04

Splats
Splat 05

Splats
Splat 06

Splats
Splat 07

Stars
Star 01

Stars
Star 02

Stars
Star 03

Stars
Star 04

Stars
Star 05

**Third
Dimension**
3D Shape 01

**Third
Dimension**
3D Shape 02

**Third
Dimension**
3D Shape 03

**Third
Dimension**
3D Shape 04

**Third
Dimension**
3D Shape 05

ShapeArt

**Third
Dimension**
3D Shape 06

**Third
Dimension**
3D Shape 07

**Third
Dimension**
3D Shape 08

**Third
Dimension**
3D Shape 09

**Third
Dimension**
3D Shape 10

**Third
Dimension**
3D Shape 11

**Third
Dimension**
3D Shape 12

**Third
Dimension**
3D Shape 13

**Third
Dimension**
3D Shape 14

**Third
Dimension**
3D Shape 15

**Third
Dimension**
3D Shape 16

**Third
Dimension**
3D Shape 17

**Third
Dimension**
3D Shape 18

**Third
Dimension**
3D Shape 19

**Third
Dimension**
3D Shape 20

**Third
Dimension**
3D Shape 21

**Third
Dimension**
3D Shape 22

**Third
Dimension**
3D Shape 23

**Third
Dimension**
3D Shape 24

**Third
Dimension**
3D Shape 25

**Third
Dimension**
3D Shape 26

**Third
Dimension**
3D Shape 27

**Third
Dimension**
3D Shape 28

**Third
Dimension**
3D Shape 29

**Third
Dimension**
3D Shape 30

Design Templates

3

Introduction

Design Templates

This section covers the Design Templates included with the **DrawPlus X2 Resource CD**. These can be accessed from the **Startup Wizard** and include the sections **Arts & Crafts**, **Logos**, **Posters**, **Web Banners**, and **Greeting Cards**.

Be sure to check out the new **keyframe animation** Design Templates in the **Animated Web Banners** category!

Arts & Crafts

The **Arts & Crafts** section includes the categories **Pop-up Cards**, **Colouring In**, **Cootie Catchers**, **Paper Crafts**, **Scrapbooking**, and **Wrapping Paper**. All of these templates are interactive and are ready for you to print out and use! See the examples on the following pages. Where necessary, we have provided illustrations of how templates will look when printed, cut-out, and folded. Enjoy!

Pop-up Cards

Arts & Crafts- Pop-up Cards

Champagne

Flowers

Halloween

Arts & Crafts - Pop-up Cards

Headphones

True Love

Colouring In

Space Aliens

Farmer

Ice Cream

Pirates

Art & Crafts - Cootie Catchers

Cootie Catchers

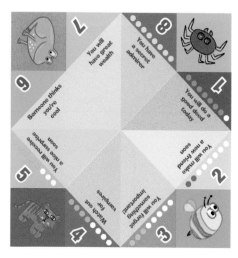

Animals

Art & Crafts - Cootie Catchers

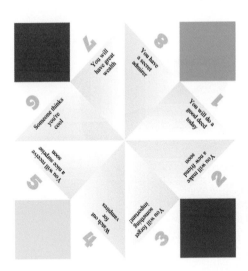

Basic

Patterns

Paper Crafts

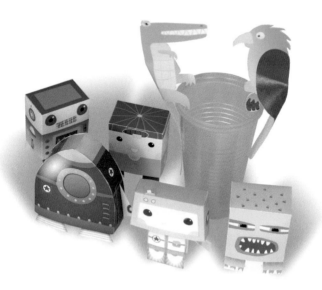

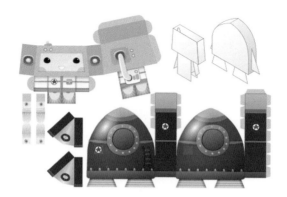

Space Toy

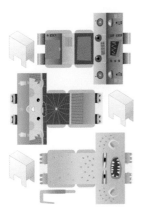

Box Toys

Cocktail Characters

Nursery Mobiles

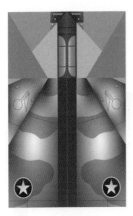

Jet Plane

Shuttle

Scrapbooking

Camping

Messy Desk

Wrapping Paper

Petals

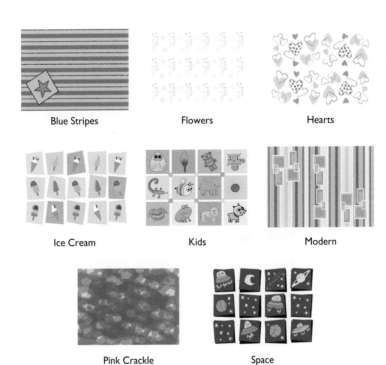

Blue Stripes

Flowers

Hearts

Ice Cream

Kids

Modern

Pink Crackle

Space

Logos

Logos

Airline

Arts

Astronomical

Banking

Bio Research

Biz

Blocks

Bookstore

Box

Button

Chess

Chivalric Order

Chocoholics

Circles

Compact Disc

Dots

Dragon Crest

Enterprise

Environmental

Financial

Firm

Formal

Fraternity

Guild

Home

Logos

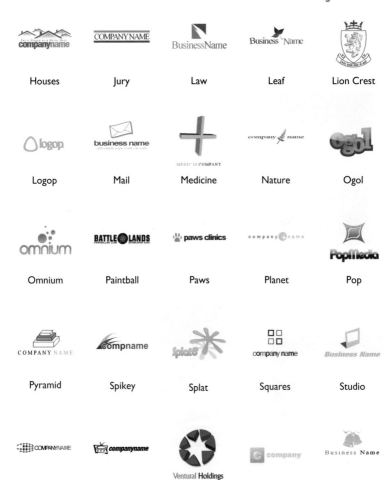

Houses

Jury

Law

Leaf

Lion Crest

Logop

Mail

Medicine

Nature

Ogol

Omnium

Paintball

Paws

Planet

Pop

Pyramid

Spikey

Splat

Squares

Studio

Tech

Television

Ventural

Web 2.0

Weddings

Weightbusters

Posters - Events

Posters

Events
African Art Show

Events
Book Store

Events
Classic Car Show

Events
Coffee Morning

Events
Country Folk

Events
Dance Event

Posters - Events / Food & Nightlife

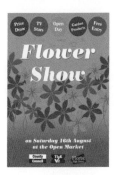

Events
Flowers Show

Events
Folk Festival

Events
Garden Festival

Events
Prom Night

Events
Record Fair

Events
Record Sale

Events
Village Fair

Food & Nightlife
Butterfly Menu

Food & Nightlife
Café Now Open

Posters - Food & Nightlife / Misc

Food & Nightlife
Dancing Club

Food & Nightlife
Drinks Offers

Food & Nightlife
Italian Restaurant

Food & Nightlife
Lounge Club

Food & Nightlife
Party Club

Food & Nightlife
Restaurant Open Soon

Misc
Action Movie

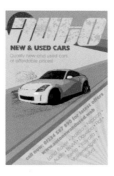

Misc
Car Sales

Misc
City At Night Movie

Misc
Education Crafts

Misc
Environment Notice

Misc
Looking For Love Movie

Misc
Performance Management
Training

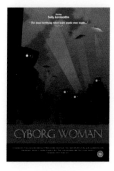

Misc
Sci-Fi Movie

Retail
Closing Down

Retail
Cruise Offer

Retail
Discount Swirly

Retail
Dressmakers

Posters - Retail

Retail
Everything Dropped

Retail
Fine Wines

Retail
Flower Bouquet

Retail
Fresh Skin Care

Retail
Music Shop

Retail
New Year Sale

Retail
Open Day

Retail
Organic Cosmetics

Retail
Shirts Spring Deals

Retail
Splash Out

Retail
Spring Sale Motif

Retail
Store Banner

Retail
Summer Collection

Retail
Sunglasses Offer

Retail
The Fruit Tree

Retail
Tropical Holidays

Retail
Urban Alternative Retail

Introduction

Web Banners

The **DrawPlus X2 Design Templates** include **Animated Web Banners and Static Web Banners** sections.

Both animated and static web banners are easy to insert into and modify on your own Web pages!

Web Banners - Animated

Animated Web Banners are **keyframe animation** documents—our example below illustrates various stages of the animation—why not open one and preview it for yourself?

Web Banners - Animated - Landscape

Chocoholics

College

Green Solutions

Holiday Adventures

Outdoors

Red City

Regina

Web Banners - Animated - Landscape / Portrait

Restaurant

Tricore

Web Banners - Animated - Portrait

College   Chocoholics   Epoc Solutions   Outdoors

Web Banners - Animated - Portrait / Static - Landscape

Restaurant

Web Hosting

Web Banners - Static - Landscape

Animals

Casino

Digital Camera

Digital Media

Web Banners - Static - Landscape

Estate Agents

Green Solutions

Health & Beauty

Lunar Eclipse

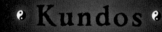

Martial Arts

Music

Orange Orb

Tricore

Web Hosting

Web Banners - Static - Landscape / Portrait

Wine

xytron

Web Banners - Static - Portrait

Animals

Casino

Digital Camera

Digital Media

Web Banners - Static - Portrait

Estate Agents

Green Solutions

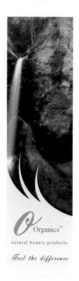

Health & Beauty

Lunar Eclipse

Luxury Hotel

Martial Arts

Music

Orange Orb

Web Banners - Static - Portrait

Tricore

Web Hosting

Wine

xytron

Greeting Cards

Birthday
Animals

Birthday
Bees

Birthday
Dinosaur

Birthday
Elephants

Birthday
Footballer

Birthday
Frog

Birthday
Gardener

Birthday
Guitar

Birthday
Motorbike

Birthday
Party

Birthday
Rugby

Birthday
Sunflower

Birthday
Tennis

Birthday
Trees

Christmas
Bauble

Christmas
Christmas
Cheer

Christmas
Christmas Pud

Christmas
Christmas
Puddings

Christmas
Mistletoe

Christmas
Nativity

Christmas
Robin

Christmas
Santa

Christmas
Snowflakes

Christmas
Snowman

Occasions
Abstract
Canvas

Greeting Cards

Occasions
Baby Boy

Occasions
Baby Girl

Occasions
Ballerina
Thanks

Occasions
Be My
Valentine

Occasions
Champagne

Occasions
Circles

Occasions
Congratulations
Wedding Cake

Occasions
Cute Hearts

Occasions
Easter Egg

Occasions
First Day at
School

Occasions
Get Well
Soon Teddy

Occasions
Graduation

Occasions
Halloween

Occasions
I Love You

Occasions
I'm Sorry

Occasions
Just Married

Occasions
Leaving
Rooster

Occasions
New Arrival
Bunnies

Occasions
Mothers Day

Occasions
Passed Driving
Test

Occasions
Relax

Occasions
Retirement

Occasions
Sorry

Occasions
Thank You

Design Elements

4

Introduction

DrawPlus provides an exciting range of possibilities for creating natural looking artistic effects using natural media effect brushstrokes and a selection of coordinated themed palettes.

On the **Brushes** tab, you'll find a range of new and improved pressure-sensitive brush strokes that allow you to create pencil sketches, charcoal drawings, pen and ink sketches, watercolours, and more.

On the **Swatches** tab, we've included additional themed palettes—for example, **Acrylics**, **Art Spectrum**, and **Artist's Colours**—specially designed with the artist in mind. The **Swatches** tab also provides a wide selection of **Gradient** and **Bitmap Fills**, which you can apply with a single click and then modify to suit your needs.

On the **Effects** tab, choose from an extensive range of powerful preset **Instant Effects**—improved and extended for DrawPlus X2.

Get to grips with these design elements and you'll dramatically expand your potential for creativity!

Brushes

Charcoal

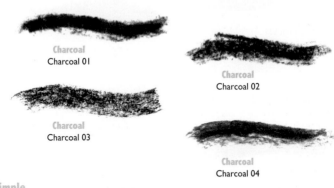

Charcoal
Charcoal 01

Charcoal
Charcoal 02

Charcoal
Charcoal 03

Charcoal
Charcoal 04

Simple

Simple
Airbrush

Simple
Circle

Simple
Hard Circle

Simple
Hard Taper

Simple
Soft Airbrush

Simple
Soft Taper

Simple
Taper

Brushes - Dry Paint

Dry Paint

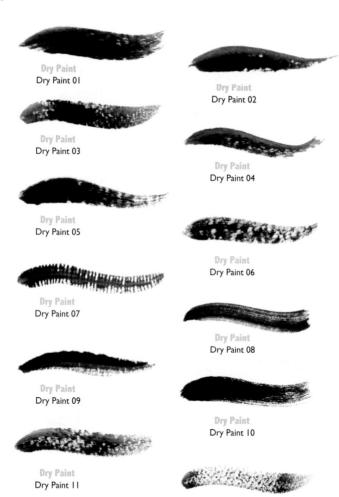

Dry Paint
Dry Paint 01

Dry Paint
Dry Paint 02

Dry Paint
Dry Paint 03

Dry Paint
Dry Paint 04

Dry Paint
Dry Paint 05

Dry Paint
Dry Paint 06

Dry Paint
Dry Paint 07

Dry Paint
Dry Paint 08

Dry Paint
Dry Paint 09

Dry Paint
Dry Paint 10

Dry Paint
Dry Paint 11

Dry Paint
Dry Paint 12

Dry Paint
Dry Paint 13

Felt Tip

Felt Tip
Felt Tip 01

Felt Tip
Felt Tip 02

Felt Tip
Felt Tip 03

Felt Tip
Felt Tip 04

Felt Tip
Felt Tip 05

Felt Tip
Felt Tip 06

Medium Paint

Medium Paint
Medium Paint 01

Medium Paint
Medium Paint 02

Medium Paint
Medium Paint 03

Medium Paint
Medium Paint 04

Medium Paint
Medium Paint 05

Medium Paint
Medium Paint 06

Medium Paint
Medium Paint 07

Brushes - Medium Paint / Pastel

Medium Paint
Medium Paint 09

Medium Paint
Medium Paint 08

Medium Paint
Medium Paint 10

Medium Paint
Medium Paint 11

Pastel

Pastel
Pastel 01

Pastel
Pastel 02

Pastel
Pastel 03

Pastel
Pastel 04

Pastel
Pastel 05

Pastel
Pastel 06

Pastel
Pastel 07

Pen

Pen
Pen 01

Pen
Pen 02

Pen
Pen 03

Pen
Pen 04

Pen
Pen 05

Pen
Pen 06

Pen
Pen 07

Pen
Pen 08

Pen
Pen 09

Pen
Pen 10

Pen
Pen 11

Pencil

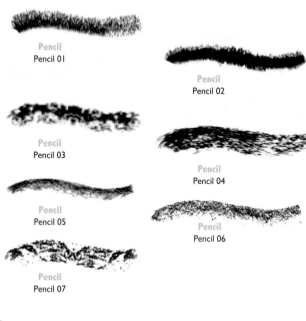

Pencil
Pencil 01

Pencil
Pencil 02

Pencil
Pencil 03

Pencil
Pencil 04

Pencil
Pencil 05

Pencil
Pencil 06

Pencil
Pencil 07

Photo

Photo
Chain2

Photo
Garden Shovel

Photo
Green Chilli Pepper

Photo
Knife

Photo
Music

Photo
Picture Frame

Photo
Rolling Pin

Photo
Scarf

Photo
String

Texture

Texture
Texture 01

Texture
Texture 02

Texture
Texture 03

Texture
Texture 04

Texture
Texture 05

Texture
Texture 06

Texture
Texture 07

Texture
Texture 08

Texture
Texture 09

Texture
Texture 10

Brushes - Texture / Watery Paint

Texture
Texture 11

Texture
Texture 12

Texture
Texture 13

Watery Paint

Watery Paint
Watery Paint 01

Watery Paint
Watery Paint 02

Watery Paint
Watery Paint 03

Watery Paint
Watery Paint 04

Watery Paint
Watery Paint 05

Watery Paint
Watery Paint 06

Watery Paint
Watery Paint 07

Watery Paint
Watery Paint 08

Watery Paint
Watery Paint 09

Watery Paint
Watery Paint 10

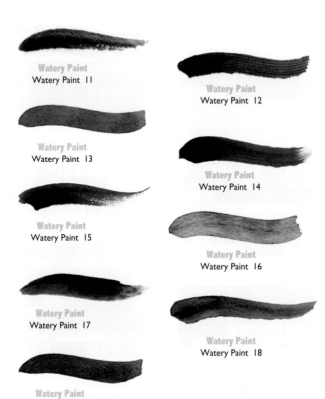

Watery Paint
Watery Paint 11

Watery Paint
Watery Paint 12

Watery Paint
Watery Paint 13

Watery Paint
Watery Paint 14

Watery Paint
Watery Paint 15

Watery Paint
Watery Paint 16

Watery Paint
Watery Paint 17

Watery Paint
Watery Paint 18

Watery Paint
Watery Paint 19

Palettes

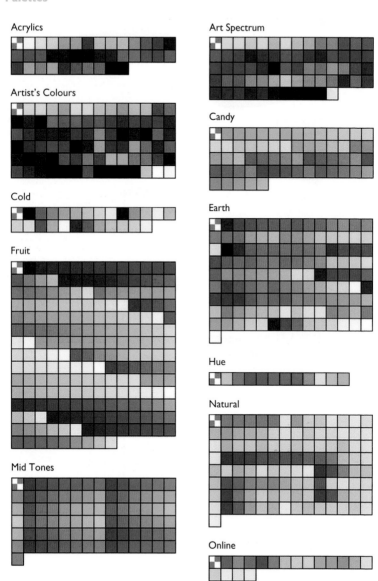

Acrylics

Art Spectrum

Artist's Colours

Candy

Cold

Earth

Fruit

Hue

Natural

Mid Tones

Online

Pastels

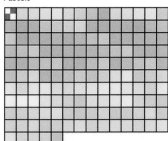

Soft Tones

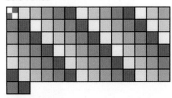

Standard RGB

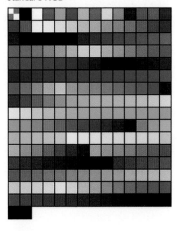

Warmth

Rainbow

Standard CYMK

Wild

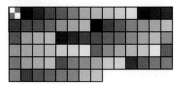

Samples

5

Introduction

Samples

To demonstrate the incredible flexibility of DrawPlus, we've provided you with a varied collection of sample documents. From realistic media effects, created with the new natural media brushes, through to posters and animation, these designs show you some of the effects you can achieve. We hope they'll inspire you to create your own works of art.

Dancing Club

Space Aliens

Dressmakers

Ice Cream

Party Club

Pirates

Village Fair

Alien Alone

Bruiser George

Come Back Soon

Concert Poster

Floral Escape

Go Ski

Little Devil Billy

Mum Son and Dog

Sports Car

Office Daydream

Portrait

Robot Convention
2020

Space Boys

Space Child

The Tree of
Forgotten Guilt

Watercolour

Pastel City

Bird on a Rock

Bridge

Dog

Electricity

Fishing

Still Life

Toucan

World Window

Bass Synth

Bike

Drinks On Us

Electric Fan

Samples / Animations

Golf

Radio Days

Shark

Technical

Watch

Scooter

Keyframe Animations

Jigsaw

Boxes

Stopframe Animations

Radio Days

Shark

Technical

Notes

Notes

Notes

Notes